FOLLYFOOT PONY QUIZ BOOK

By the same author in Piccolo

A PONY SCRAPBOOK
A SECOND PONY SCRAPBOOK

FOLLYFOOT PONY QUIZ BOOK

CHRISTINE PULLEIN-THOMPSON

Anagrams and Crosswords by
Charlotte Popescu

Line drawings by David McKee

A PICCOLO ORIGINAL

PAN BOOKS LTD
LONDON AND SYDNEY

First published 1974 by Pan Books Ltd,
Cavaye Place, London SW10 9PG

ISBN 0 330 23969 4

2nd Printing 1974

The name FOLLYFOOT is used with the kind permission
of Monica Dickens and Yorkshire Television Ltd

*Printed and bound in England by
Cox & Wyman Ltd,
London, Reading and Fakenham*

LIST OF CONTENTS

Caring for a Pony

Story Puzzle

Why did Merlin get so thin?

Sally rose early every morning to feed Merlin before she left for school. She put two pounds of potato peelings in a bag and ran quickly down the garden path to where he was anxiously waiting. It was January and the small paddock was white with frost. After tipping the potato peelings over the fence, Sally hastened to break the ice on the water. She gave Merlin a quick kiss before rushing in to get ready for school. In the evening she took him a shopping bag full of hay and several cabbage leaves. She broke the ice again by torch light. She gave him the same amount of food every day, only sometimes giving him carrot peelings instead of cabbage leaves. By the middle of February Merlin was very thin and Sally started giving him a cupful of porridge oats every morning. By the 21st of February he appeared very weak and an Inspector from the RSPCA called to say that he had been sent by the police and would be suing Sally's parents for cruelty to animals.

What had Sally done wrong? Why did Merlin get so thin?

Quiz 2

Which One Fits?

1. About how much hay should a small pony be fed every day in winter:
   (a) 3 lbs?
   (b) 12 lbs? ✓
   (c) 30 lbs?

2. If your pony won't be caught, should you:
   (a) Starve him until he will?
   (b) Get friends to help round him up and then give him a thrashing?
   (c) Take a bucket of oats and stay in the field until he's caught; then leave a headcollar on with a piece of rope attached?

3. When you groom your pony, should you begin by:
   (a) Brushing his tail?
   (b) Picking out his hoofs?
   (c) Sponging his eyes and nostrils?

4. Is hogging:
   (a) A kind of wisping?
   (b) Not letting anyone else near your pony?
   (c) Clipping off a mane?

5. Should linseed be:
   (a) Boiled for a long time before feeding?
   (b) Fed as an oil?
   (c) Fed dry?

6. Are day-old lawn clippings:
   (a) Good for a pony?
   (b) Better than hay?
   (c) Liable to cause colic?

7. If your pony is living out in winter, should you:
   (a) Clip him?
   (b) Blanket-clip him in January?
   (c) Leave him as he is?

8. Is a bang tail:
   (a) A tail which has been permed?
   (b) A tail cut squarely at hock level?
   (c) A tail doubled under and knotted for polo matches?

9. Is chaff:
   (a) Chopped hay or straw to mix in feeds?
   (b) A kind of barley?
   (c) Slang for dirty bedding?

10. Should hay be coloured:
    (a) Yellow?
    (b) Greenish-brownish?
    (c) Blackish-brownish?

Picture Puzzle

These 4 riders are all trying to get home after a long ride. Can you find which rider belongs to which house?

A-4   B-2   C-1   D-3

Quiz 4

Odd One Out

One word or phrase in each line doesn't fit. Can you find it?

1. Clover, Sanfoin, Mixture, Silage.
2. Oats, Barley, Meadow, Wheat.
3. Broken, Crushed, Rolled, Bruised.
4. Oats, Bran, Pony nuts, Hay.
5. Trimming, Washing, Clipping, Schooling.
6. Blanket, Foot, Full, Trace.
7. Pulling, Plaiting, Wrenching, Hogging.
8. Rack up, Sack up, Rug up, Stack up.
9. Strapping, Quartering, Wisping, Kicking.
10. Gates, Fences, Water, Roads.
11. Flour, Beans, Maize, Linseed.
12. Gently, Firmly, Calmly, Hysterically.

Quiz 5

Right or Wrong?

Some of these statements are right, and some wrong. Can you tell which are which?

1. A pony coming in hot from a ride should be cooled by a fast gallop round the field.
2. A stabled pony should have his hoofs picked out at least once a day.
3. You should give your pony hot water in winter to keep him warm.
4. A lame pony needs plenty of exercise to make his legs strong.
5. An ill pony should be kept warm.
6. The vet should be called to a pony suffering from jaundice.
7. Musty hay is the best hay for a pony with bronchitis.
8. A pony should not be ridden if he's coughing.
9. A pony needs a long cool drink after a large feed.
10. A pony should always be fed hay in winter.
11. Ponies need shade or a shelter in their field during the summer months.
12. A pony which hunts regularly needs two tons of oats a month.

Pair Them Up
Do you know which of these words go together?

BRAN   CRUSHED   CLIP

    FULL   MANE   TACK

        BANG   OUT

     OUT   DOWN

LICK

     MASH   OATS   FLAKED

  UP   HOGGED

   PONY   BOILED

      RUB   TURN

MAIZE

    LINSEED   RUG

      TAIL

CLIP   MUCK

   NUTS   UP   TRACE

         SALT

Quiz 7

Fill in the Missing Words

choosing from amongst those at the bottom of the page

1. When the weather is very cold you must break the .... on your pony's water.
2. A clipped pony needs .... in winter.
3. Every pony needs one .... off from work a week.
4. When you turn a pony out in a new field, you should always check the ....
5. If your pony is wet, you should .... his back before putting the saddle on.
6. Fat, unfit ponies should not be ....
7. Two-year-old ponies should .... be ridden.
8. Thoroughbreds should .... live out in winter without a shelter.
9. You should feed your pony at least .... a day in winter.
10. You should look at your pony .... day all the year round.

ice   numb   galloped   every   sometimes   fences
plumb   not   day   summer   rugs   skinny   dry
clumsy   never   twice

Quiz 8

Anagrams

1. NELDEIS.
2. TLERHA.
3. LTDASEB.
4. NREHTU PLCI.
5. EFNEC.
6. KGUCMIN TOU.
7. ANBR SMHA.
8. RNOGIMOG.
9. FHAFC.
10. TRIGSAN AOCT.

Quiz 9

Sort Them Out

In each section some suggestions are true, some are false. Can you pick out the true ones?

1. *Suitable food for your pony:*
   Pony nuts? Wheat straw? Mixture hay? Grass? Potato peelings? Chopped carrot? Crushed oats? Dry flaked maize? Breakfast cereals? Acorn pulp?

2. *Suitable grooming tools:*
   Your own hair brush? Dandy brush? Water brush? Tooth brush? Wire brush? Body brush? Kitchen broom? Stable rubber? Daddy's screw driver? Curry comb?

3. *Suitable for tack cleaning:*
   Lavender scented silicone spray? Saddle soap? Sponges? Jeyes Fluid? Parazone bleach? Neatsfoot oil? Metal polish? Soft duster? Shaving brush? Dishcloth?

4. *Suitable place for your pony to live:*
   Kitchen garden? Greenhouse? Loose box? Hen run? Farmer's field? Toolshed? Shady paddock? Stable? Orchard (spring and winter)? Tethered on front lawn?

5. *Suitable treatment for pony all the year round:*
   Clip in March? Bring in all day in summer? Visit every day? Call blacksmith to examine shoes every

three months? Pick out hoofs before riding? Examine shoes regularly? Wash daily in winter? Clean his tack regularly? Ride with mud under the saddle? Clip in August?

6. *Suitable treatment for pony's paddock:*
   Remove dung? Keep water trough clean? Use weedkiller on weeds? Cut ragwort and leave to die? Put salt in drinking water to kill germs? Inspect fences regularly? Fill up rabbit holes? Remove all clover? Pick up garbage and sharp stones? Replace hedges with barbed wire?

7. *Suitable for stable bedding:*
   Hay? Peat? Grass? Sawdust? Wood shavings? Compost? Wheat straw? Lawn mowings? Old sacks? Oat straw?

8. *Suitable treatment for thin pony:*
   Feed quantities of granulated sugar? Increase food? Worm? Feed raw potatoes? Get teeth examined? Send to knackers? Ride more to increase appetite? Have examined by vet? Feed boiled linseed, soaked flaked maize and boiled barley? Send to market as useless?

9. *Suitable food for old pony with loose teeth:*
   Split beans? Meadow hay? Whole oats? Grass? Crushed oats? Bran? Extra vitamins? Mangolds? Clover hay? Wheat?

10. *Suitable treatment for very fat pony:*
    Give less food? Give only oats? Ride regularly? Gallop to make him sweat? Bring in every day in summer? Give clover hay? Put in smaller field? Feed boiled barley? Ride slowly until thinner? Give no food for three days?

Competing—Showing, Cross Country, Show Jumping, Gymkhanas

Quiz 10

Story Puzzle
Should Ann have won her rosettes?

Ann rose early on the morning of the gymkhana and plaited her pony Sinbad. Her father had the trailer ready hitched to the car and by ten o'clock Ann was cantering round the showground with her friends. Her first event was Bending, and she soon found herself in the final; she knocked down a pole but still finished three yards ahead of the others and was awarded the first rosette. In the potato race, she missed the bucket with the last potato, but, jumping off, threw it in, put up her arm and was again awarded first prize. Finally came the musical poles, and soon Ann was competing with three others for the last two poles. When the music stopped she galloped in, grabbed a pole but was going so fast that she couldn't hold on to it. A small girl on a skewbald seized it, but the judge insisted that since Ann touched the pole first, the other girl must go out, which she did protesting loudly. Sally was out next time, but was still awarded the second rosette.

Should Ann have been awarded these three rosettes? And if not, why not? Do you know?

Quiz 11

Which One Fits?

1. If you start before the bell in a big jumping event, are you:
   (a) Eliminated?
   (b) Given time faults?
   (c) Allowed to go back and begin again?

2. How much must a show jumper have won in prize money to become a Grade B horse:
   (a) Fifty pounds?
   (b) One hundred and fifty pounds?
   (c) Twenty pounds?

3. If you canter in a Trotting race, should you:
   (a) Turn a circle and continue?
   (b) Consider yourself disqualified and leave the ring?
   (c) Hope the judges haven't noticed and continue at a trot?

4. Is the Coffin jump likely to be found at:
   (a) Wembley?
   (b) Hickstead?
   (c) Badminton?

5. If you had an Exmoor pony, which class would you show him in:
   (a) Working Pony?

(b) Mountain and Moorland?

(c) Hack?

6. What is the minimum age for competitors in Nations Cups, Grand Prix or Puissance competitions:
   (a) 14?
   (b) 18?
   (c) 21?

7. Is a bogey time in Hunter Trials:
   (a) A special correct time set before the event to help decide the winner?
   (b) A time limit?
   (c) The fastest time possible in which to complete the course?

8. How much weight must a show jumper carry in an International jumping competition:
   (a) 12 st?
   (b) 9 st 8 lbs?
   (c) 11 st 11 lbs?

9. Is the Golden Horse Shoe Ride:
   (a) A track across the Pennines?
   (b) A trail competition in California?
   (c) A competitive long distance ride held in Britain?

10. If you are asked to lead your pony in a Showing Class, should you:
    (a) Take the reins over his head and run in front hoping he will follow?
    (b) Take the reins over his head and run with him on the nearside?
    (c) Use your whip to make him lively and then run like a hare?

Picture Puzzle

Which of these jumps are not found in the show-jumping ring?

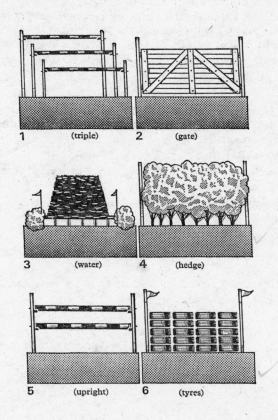

1   (triple)

2   (gate)

3   (water)

4   (hedge)

5   (upright)

6   (tyres)

Odd One Out

One word or phrase in every line doesn't fit. Can you find it?

1. Bending, Flag, Mug, Spoon and Fork.
2. Hit and hurry, Get on and off, Scurry, Local.
3. Hog's back, Rustic poles, Vanguard, Wall.
4. Family, Working, Leading rein, Ordinary.
5. There and back, Run and lead, Sack, Trotting.
6. Grade A, Grade G, Grade B, Grade C.
7. Hunter trials, Horse trials, Eventing, Jumping at Hickstead.
8. Iceland, Italy, Spain, Britain.
9. Musical chairs, Musical poles, Musical paperbags, Musical sacks.
10. Relay, Pairs, Horse and groom, Apple bobbing.
11. Water jump, Open ditch, River, Combination.
12. Cross bars, Triple, Parallel bars, Gate.

Quiz 14

Right or Wrong?

Some of these statements are right and some wrong. Do you know which are which?

1. There is a team jumping competition for schools at Hickstead.
2. Anyone who is good can be in a Prince Philip Team.
3. Most show jumpers have reached their peak by the time they are six.
4. There is a cross-country competition for boys under sixteen at Badminton.
5. You cannot Point-to-point unless your horse has been hunted.
6. Mountain and Moorland ponies are often shown unplaited.
7. Hunters and hacks are often shown ridden side saddle.
8. You need a top hat to compete in very advanced dressage tests.
9. A leading rein pony is always led when shown.
10. If you lose your hat and jump without it, you are eliminated in Pony Club Horse Trials.
11. Going past a flag on the wrong side does not matter in Hunter Trials.
12. You don't need a hard hat when riding in gymkhana events.

Pair Them Up

Do you know which of these words go together?

HUNTER   POLES

                 JUMPING   RACE

    APPLE   FALSE   ENTRY

      BRONZE   MUSICAL

   MEDAL   TRIALS

         MUG   BOBBING

STEEPLE   CUP

    ROUND   CHASING

      SCURRY   HANDY

CHALLENGE   TEETH

        LATE   RING

RUSTIC   COLLECTING   SACKS

   SHARK'S   START

      HUNTER

       CLEAR

Quiz 16

Fill in the Missing Words

choosing from amongst those at the bottom of the page

1. In a Handy Hunter you may have to .... a gate.
2. In a showing class you may have to take your .... off.
3. The Hickstead .... is one of the biggest jumping events at Hickstead.
4. The Prince Philip Teams compete in their finals at ....
5. There are .... members in a Prince Philip Team.
6. In Horse Trials the horses do a dressage test, go across country and jump some ....
7. In show jumping a refusal counts as .... faults.
8. If you turn your back on a jump it counts as a ....
9. If you have three refusals you are ....
10. At a big show it is best to wear a black or navy .... and .... in a showing class.
11. In a show jumping ring two or more jumps close together are called a ....
12. A minimus Gymkhana is usually for ....riders.

combination leggings saddle carrot five
coat sack eliminated show jumps first
gloves refusal elderly three faults forty
open Wembley Garden party young Derby

Quiz 17

Anagrams

1. HWSO GIRN.
2. RPETIL.
3. LESHUECD.
4. GMNUIJP.
5. TIDHKECAS.
6. NAERA.
7. ISRHI KBNA.
8. SPITLA.
9. NUBLCILFH.
10. TEWRA MUPJ.

Quiz 18

Sort Them Out

In each section some suggestions are true, some false. Can you pick out the true ones?

1. *Gymkhana events:*
   Sack race? Fancy dress? Take off your shoes race? Bending race? Backwards race? Catch a fly race? Musical poles? Trotting race? Catch your pony race? Mug race?

2. *Usual jumping competitions:*
   Lead jumping? Novice jumping? Local jumping? Green pony jumping? Scurry competition? Hit and hurry? Run and jump? Open jumping? Career jumping? Infant jumping?

3. *Pony Showing Classes:*
   Mountain and Moorland? First pony? Leading rein? Family pony? Pony cob? Second pony? Working pony? Best child's pony not over 13.2? Best gymkhana pony? Best show jumper under 13.2?

4. *Horse Showing Classes:*
   Best three cobs? Hunter? Hack? Working hunter? Working Dressage horse? High school horse? Brood mare? Arab? Race horse? Charger?

5. *For showing, a pony needs:*
To be plaited? A straight cut saddle? A pair of rubber coloured reins? Clean tack? A saddle cloth? A yellow browband? To lead in hand? A tidy rider? Bandages? A drop noseband?

6. *A working hunter needs:*
A numnah? A twisted snaffle? A double bridle? A running martingale? To be plaited? To jump? To be well groomed? Very short legs? A good rider? Over-reach boots?

7. *In gymkhana events you will find:*
Apples? Buckets? Nails? Hammers? Poles? Potatoes? Cabbages? Mouth organs? Flags? Wire?

8. *More gymkhana events:*
Run and lead? Balloon race? Flower race? Stepping stones? Hit the headlines race? Fall and run? Dressing-up race? Anti-litter race? Grandparents' race? Three legged race?

9. *Movements found in an easy Dressage Test:*
A serpentine? A piaffe? Circles? Leads off on either leg? Full passes at a canter? Flying changes every third stride? Standing still? Ordinary trot sitting? Counter leads? Vaulting on at a gallop?

10. *Likely jumps in the show ring:*
Brick and cement wall? Sand bank? Water jump? Rustic poles? Thorn hedge? Gate? Barbed wire? Road closed? String jump? Triple?

Equitation – Riding and Schooling

Quiz 19

Story Puzzle
Why did Twilight stop jumping?

Lisa was a conceited child. Her parents had recently paid four hundred pounds for a pony called Twilight, which could jump five foot. Lisa was determined to win all the prizes at the local shows on Twilight. She imagined her room full of silver cups, her photograph in the papers. Her father paid ninety pounds for a set of painted show jumps. The month was August, hot and fine, with never a cloud in the sky, and Lisa schooled Twilight over these jumps day after day, raising them a little each time, though never bothering to change the actual course. Her father watched cheering her on, while the ground grew harder and the grass more parched. Then two days before Lisa's first show, Twilight stopped jumping. She refused again and again and no amount of beating could make her jump anything but the smallest jump.

What had Lisa done wrong? Why did Twilight stop jumping?

Quiz 20

Which One Fits?

1. Is lunging:
   (a) A horse which lunges towards you?
   (b) Sending a horse round on a circle at the end of a long rein?
   (c) Riding a horse in side reins?

2. Are Aids:
   (a) Signals you use to guide and direct your pony?
   (b) Hats, crops, whips, spurs?
   (c) The same as first aid?

3. Is a Cavaletti:
   (a) A long whip?
   (b) A type of martingale?
   (c) A pole mounted on X shaped ends, used for jumping?

4. Is a free walk:
   (a) The walk of a loose horse?
   (b) The walk of a ridden horse on a long, loose rein?
   (c) A ride you don't pay for?

5. Is a flying change:
   (a) Changing horses without dismounting, preferably at the gallop?

    (b) Flying horses from one competition to another?

    (c) When a horse changes leg in mid air?

6. If your pony is only three, should you:
   (a) Ride him a lot?
   (b) Start riding him gently when he is four?
   (c) Ride him only at week-ends?

7. Is a practise jump:
   (a) A jump put up at a show for you to practise over before competing?
   (b) A jump you practise over all day at home?
   (c) A narrow jump without wings used for schooling?

8. If your pony is frightened of a bus, should you:
   (a) Beat him until he goes past?
   (b) Swear at the bus driver?
   (c) Ask the driver to stop the bus, calm your pony and then ride slowly past?

9. Is the Spanish Walk:
   (a) A high school movement?
   (b) Something horses do at a bull fight?
   (c) The dance of an Arab stallion?

10. When you are riding should you:
    (a) Look straight ahead?
    (b) Look at your pony's legs to see whether they are working properly?
    (c) Look for things jumping out of hedges?

Picture Puzzle

See how many letters you can mark in on this small-sized dressage arena.

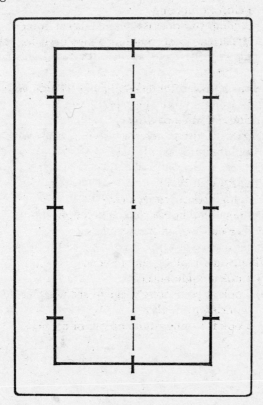

Quiz 22

Odd One Out
One word or phrase in every line doesn't fit. Can you find it?

1. Canter, Trot, Gallop, Stop.
2. Vault, Mount, Somersault, Dismount.
3. Ordinary, Collected, Extended, Peculiar.
4. Legs, Hands, Voice, Spurs.
5. Half-halt, Half-rear, Turn on the haunches, Shoulder-in.
6. Rearing, Bucking, Bolting, Flexing.
7. Stargazing, Resisting the bit, Head throwing, Dropping the nose.
8. Balanced, Cadenced, Calmly, Stiffly.
9. Quietly, Confidently, Lazily, Determinedly.
10. Shying, Jibbing, Napping, Balanced.
11. On the bit, Behind the bit, Resisting the bit, Ignoring the bit.
12. Changes of rein, Circles, Changes of direction, Long gallops.

Quiz 23

Right or Wrong?

Some of these statements are right, and some wrong. Do you know which are which?

1. A dressage horse must be well-schooled.
2. You should sit on the cantle of your saddle.
3. Shoulder-in is a suppling exercise.
4. The walk is a one time gait.
5. Dressage horses are not expected to canter on both legs.
6. Your hands should be as high as your waist when you are schooling.
7. A pony needs schooling for four hours a day if he's to learn dressage.
8. To rein back is to move backwards.
9. When halting, a pony should never stand squarely on all four legs.
10. A green pony is the same as a young unschooled pony.
11. A pony jumps better if he is well-schooled.
12. Jumping the same obstacle over and over again sours a pony.

Pair Them Up
Do you know which of these words go together?

SPREAD   REIN

    AIDS   TROT   FALLING

FENCE   UP   RISING

    LUNGE   CANTER

OFF   REIN

    BACK

        LEG   OUT

      BIT   IN   ARTIFICIAL

SCHOOL

    COLLECTED   COUNTER

      MASTER   CHANGE

   GROUND   MOUTHING

     RUN   LINE

    CANTER

FLYING   BREAKING

Quiz 25

Fill in the Missing Words

choosing from amongst those at the bottom of the page

1. When you are riding, you should keep your heels ....
2. Signals to your pony by hand, legs, and voice are called ....
3. When you canter a circle your pony should lead on the .... leg.
4. A 'free walk' means that your pony walks on a .... rein.
5. A pony which hits you on the nose when you are riding, needs a standing ....
6. Spurs, whips and martingales are called .... aids.
7. A trot when you don't rise is called a .... trot.
8. A good rider .... his pony when he has gone well.
9. You should never .... your temper with your pony.
10. Riding without .... is good for your seat.

out   stirrups   inside   whispering   martingale
bit   sitting   running   artificial   loose   trousers
down   sings   lose   aids   tomorrow   cold
rewards

Anagrams

1. GTIROTNT.
2. ERNI-CAKB.
3. IDSA.
4. LARLY.
5. MJSUP.
6. LAHF SPSA.
7. LOGLAP.
8. HOSDEURL-NI
9. RCIELC.
10. TECNAR.

Quiz 27

Sort Them Out

In each section some suggestions are true, some are false. Can you pick out the true ones?

1. *A good rider:*
   Loses his temper? Is kind but firm? Uses his whip a lot? Has heels lower than toes? Kicks his pony along? Looks between his pony's ears? Sits straight without being stiff? Makes wild cowboy noises? Uses his brains? Gallops all the time?

2. *Schooling should:*
   Improve your pony? Teach him circus tricks? Make him balanced? Make him cunning? Make him easier to ride? Make him faster? Make him better at competitions? Increase his value? Make him lazy? Make him grow?

3. *A pony pulls because he:*
   Has a hard mouth? Needs a curb bit? Is old? Needs schooling? Is badly ridden? Needs a good hiding? Has wrongly adjusted bit? Needs more oats? Wants a friend? Is too strong for his rider?

4. *A pony refuses to jump because he:*
   Lacks training? Has too short legs? Is sore or lame? Is constantly jagged in the mouth? Hates

his rider carrying a hunting crop? Wants a new field? Can't jump such a big fence? Needs more sugar to keep him going? Is being ridden by a nervous rider? Has a small rider?

5. *A pony bucks because:*
His saddle pinches? Your hands are too high? He doesn't like your new boots? He needs less exercise? He suffers from a cold back? He's had too many oats? He's got jaundice? He wants his own way? He's hot? He needs more exercise?

6. *Suitable schooling exercises:*
Turns on the haunches? Rearing? Circling? Running backwards? Playing at rodeos? Turns on the forehand? Racing? Stopping and starting? Sitting two on a pony? Half halts?

7. *Different kinds of trotting:*
Hanging back? Rising? Ordinary? False? Collected? Frozen? Extended? Sitting? Backwards? Hunched?

8. *Pony vices and faults:*
Jibbing? Sleeping? Bolting? Rearing? Flexing? Napping? Striding out? Kicking other ponies? Stepping out? Trotting on?

9. *Trotting up and down hill:*
Balances your pony? Unbalances your pony? Gets your pony fit? Teaches your pony bad habits? Muscles up your pony's quarters? Teaches him to slide? Improves his tail carriage? Gets his hocks under him? Improves him for Horse Trials? Makes his head shake?

10. *A four-year-old needs:*

Quiet hacking? Really hard work? Jumping in speed competitions? Lots of slow cantering? Work he will enjoy? Taking slowly until he's five? A lot of collected work? Plenty of leg? Jumping at all the big shows? Not too much of anything until he's five?

Famous Names – Equine and Human

Story Puzzle
Why was it only a dream?

Ann Moore was talking to Sir Alfred Munnings.

'Please will you paint my horses?' she asked. 'I would like a portrait of each as soon as possible to give to my mother.'

Meanwhile, Anna Sewell was sitting on the grass writing the last chapter of her book, *My Friend Flicka*.

'How on earth shall I end it, Ann?' she asked, 'I'm completely stuck. I don't want Flicka to die.'

Ann looked at her in surprise.

'All horses die in the end,' she said. 'Ask Sir Alfred Munnings to do the illustrations.'

'They must have docked tails and bearing reins,' Anna replied.

'But they were banned years ago,' said Ann. 'Didn't you know? And why are you wearing such long clothes?'

But now Anna Sewell and Sir Alfred Munnings disappeared and Ann Moore woke up with a jerk. It was only a dream, she thought. It couldn't have happened in real life anyway.

Why not? Why couldn't Ann Moore be talking to Sir Alfred Munnings and Anna Sewell?

Which One Fits?

1. Does Ann Moore jump:
   (a) Psalm?
   (b) Manhatten?
   (c) Penwood Forge Mill?

2. Did Nijinsky win:
   (a) The Grand National?
   (b) The Derby?
   (c) Badminton?

3. Does Alison Oliver train horses belonging to:
   (a) Lester Pigott?
   (b) Harvey Smith?
   (c) Princess Anne?

4. Is Bob Davies famous as:
   (a) A Point-to-point rider?
   (b) A horse trial rider?
   (c) A show jumper?

5. Was Brown Jack:
   (a) An infamous horse dealer?
   (b) A highwayman?
   (c) A famous racehorse?

6. Was Champion the Wonder Horse:
   - (a) Winner of the 1973 Burghley Horse Trials?
   - (b) A television star?
   - (c) A member of the Australian Olympic Team?

7. Is Lorna Johnstone:
   - (a) A dressage rider?
   - (b) A great breeder of racehorses?
   - (c) A trainer?

8. Is Raymond Brooks-Ward famous for:
   - (a) Horse trials?
   - (b) Winning the Grand National three times?
   - (c) As a television commentator?

9. Did Buffalo Bill:
   - (a) Kill the Cheyenne Chief Yellow Hand?
   - (b) Ride from Toronto to New York in twelve days?
   - (c) Found the US Cavalry?

10. Does Raimondo d'Inzeo jump for:
    - (a) Spain?
    - (b) France?
    - (c) Italy?

Quiz 30

Picture Puzzle – Muddled Names

The names of these famous people have got muddled up. Can you sort them out?

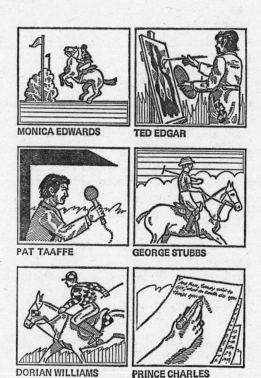

MONICA EDWARDS

TED EDGAR

PAT TAAFFE

GEORGE STUBBS

DORIAN WILLIAMS

PRINCE CHARLES

Odd One Out

One name (or title) in every line doesn't fit. Can you find it?

1. Monica Dickens, Mary O'Hara, Enid Bagnold, Esther Rantzen.
2. Mary Chapot, Bill Steinkraus, Anneli Drummond-Hay, Kathy Kusner.
3. *Wish for a Pony, Alice in Wonderland, Follyfoot, I Wanted a Pony.*
4. Anne Bullen, Norman Thelwell, Sheila Rose, Dorian Williams.
5. Tosca, Firecrest, Crusader, Snowbound.
6. Alwin Schockemohle, Ann Backhouse, Virginia Wade, Hans Gunter Winkler.
7. Beethoven, Pegasus, The Rock, Mr Banbury.
8. Ginger, Flicka, Vibart, Phantom.
9. Peter Cazalet, Gordon Richards, David Broome, Fred Winter.
10. Lester Piggott, Tommy Wade, Joe Mercer, A. Murray.
11. Richard Meade, William Carson, Mark Phillips, Richard Walker.
12. Dora, Paul, Callie, Christine.

Quiz 32

Right or Wrong?

Some of these statements are right, and some are wrong. Do you know which are which?

1. George Stubbs was a famous painter of horses.
2. David Broome was champion jockey in 1970.
3. Ann Moore won the European Ladies' Championship on Pitz Palu in 1972.
4. Harvey Smith jumps Summertime.
5. Monica Edwards wrote *Follyfoot*.
6. George Hobbs won Badminton on War Lord in 1969.
7. Richard Meade has ridden for Britain at the Olympics.
8. Badminton 1973 was won by Lucinda Prior-Palmer on Be Fair.
9. Alan Oliver was second in the Grand National last year.
10. Mary O'Hara wrote *My Friend Flicka*.
11. Pat Smythe was a famous show jumping rider.
12. Raimondo D'Inzeo jumps for Italy.

Quiz 33

Pair Them Up (*They are human!*)
Do you know which of these names go together?

WINKLER   GEORGE

       MONICA

MARK   ANN   DAVID

     SMITH   RICHARD

          MOORE

DORIAN   OLIVER

       PRINCESS

    DICKENS   MARION

MOULD

     HARVEY   BROOME

       SEWELL

         PHILLIPS

PIGGOT   WILLIAMS   DICK

    ALAN   ANNE

       STUBBS   HANS

TURPIN   ANNA

    LESTER   MEADE

Quiz 34

Fill in the Missing Words

choosing from amongst those at the bottom of the page

1. Pennwood Forge Mill is jumped by Paddy ....
2. .... Ovation competed at the Munich Olympics.
3. Lester .... has ridden many .... race winners.
4. Hideaway the famous show jumper is now usually ridden by ....
5. John Manly is a character in the book called ....
6. Napoleon rode a horse called ....
7. Warrior was a famous War Horse belonging to the painter Sir Alfred ....
8. The Maltese Cat is a .... pony in the story by Rudyard Kipling.
9. *The Three Jays* was written by famous show jumper ....
10. Duchess was the name of Black Beauty's ....

Mother Tom Jones Harvey Smith Champion
McMahon Great Ed Stewpot Munnings
Rubber Black Beauty Bumpy Polo Piggott
Tiny Pat Smythe Dr Who Marengo Turnip
Flat

Quiz 35

Anagrams

1. VADDI ORMEBO.
2. RAELK.
3. RYAM O'AHRA.
4. TBUSBS.
5. LDOBUET.
6. RMKA LHLIPSIP.
7. RETLSE GITPOTG.
8. SLAMP.
9. EGSAPSU.
10. NANA LESWEL.

Quiz 36

Sort Them Out

In each section some suggestions are true, some are false. Can you pick out the true ones?

1. *Writers of pony books:*

   Enid Blyton? Pat Smythe? Gillian Baxter? Edgar Wallace? Joanna Cannan? Dorothy Clewes? Gillian Avery? Mary Gervaise? Josephine Pullein-Thompson? Dennis Wheatley?

2. *Famous horse trial riders:*

   Richard Meade? Alan Oliver? Mary Gordon-Watson? Hans Winkler? Princess Anne? Mark Phillips? Celia Johnson? Sheila Wilcox? Norman Potter? Ann Moorehouse?

3. *Famous show jumping riders:*

   Stephen Hadley? Marion Mould? Pete Dawson? Peter Robeson? Alison Dawes? Harry Fielding? Bill Steinkraus? Johnny Deacon? Monica Edwards? Lorna Johnstone?

4. *Famous horse characters in books:*

   Merrylegs? Moonstar? Flicka? Cavalier? Black Bess? Tomtit? Snowcloud? Dr Moore? Black Knight? Mary?

5. *Famous horse experts:*
R. S. Summerhays? Mary Warner? Henry Wynmalen? Dickie Moore? The Duke of Newcastle? Caprilli? Reg Smith? Golden Gorse? Marion Rockenfeller? Adam Fry?

6. *Famous show jumpers:*
Grebe? Black Biddy? Red Admiral? Foxhunter? Susie Girl? April Love? Stroller? Ranger? Twilight? Sunstar?

7. *Famous race horses:*
Roberto? My Daddy? Nijinsky? Hyperion? Mummy's Girl? Pied Piper? Mill Reef? Golden Miller? Much Ado? Springtime?

8. *Famous cross country horses:*
Doublet? Moonstone? Cornishman V? Cheesed Off? Rock On? Be Fair? Samson? Great Ovation? Taizan? Nicolas II?

9. *Grand National winners:*
Red Alligator? Yellow Ribbon? Craven A? Highland Wedding? Red Rum? Musician? Ayala? Nightlife? Foinavon? The Banker?

10. *More famous show jumpers:*
Mr Banbury? Benjamin? Mr Softee? Cup of Tea? Top of the Morning? Daytime? Summertime? Bright Melody? Palermo? Hideaway?

Vets, Farriers and First Aid

Quiz 37

Story Puzzle
Why did Daydream die?

Daydream lived in a small paddock next to some new houses. Men were busy painting the windows of the houses. As they finished each tin of paint they threw it over the fence into the paddock.

Daydream was a very greedy pony. He would eat almost anything – polo mints, ice creams, cakes, chocolates. He belonged to a girl called Susan who was ten years old. Susan visited him when she had time, which was usually two or three times a week.

It was several days before she noticed that Daydream was ill; even then, in spite of his unhappy appearance, she waited another day before telling anyone. By then Daydream was lying down, his sides were distended and he seemed in agony. Her mother sent for the vet at once, but although he came in less than an hour, Daydream was already dead.

What did Susan do wrong? Why did Daydream die?

Which One Fits?

1. If your pony keeps rolling and kicking his stomach, should you:
   (a) Give him a large feed and hope for the best?
   (b) Give him a hot mash with Epsom salts?
   (c) Send for the vet?

2. If your pony is broken-winded, should you:
   (a) Damp his hay and only ride him gently?
   (b) Turn him out for a month and then ride him as much and as fast as possible?
   (c) Keep him stabled and feed nothing but oat straw?

3. If your pony has an itchy mane and tail, should you suspect:
   (a) Fleas?
   (b) Ringworm?
   (c) Sweet-itch?

4. If your pony has a sore back, should you:
   (a) Rest him and get an expert to see whether your saddle fits?
   (b) Rub your pony with methylated spirits and go on riding?
   (c) Put cotton wool under the saddle and continue riding?

5. If blood is gushing out of your pony's main artery, should you:
   (a) Put a bucket underneath to catch the blood?
   (b) Put a tourniquet above the wound, send for the vet immediately, and remember to release the tourniquet every fifteen minutes?
   (c) Put him in the stable, throw a bucket of cold water over the wound, then bathe with antiseptic and bandage?

6. If your pony won't eat, should you:
   (a) Try feeding sugar mixed with apple?
   (b) Starve him until he does?
   (c) Suspect illness and send for the vet?

7. If your pony casts a shoe when you are hacking, should you:
   (a) Borrow some nails and try to put it on again?
   (b) Tie some cloth over the hoof and continue riding?
   (c) Lead him home along grass verges?

8. If your pony starts weaving, is it because:
   (a) He's bored?
   (b) Too fat?
   (c) Overworked?

9. Is Strangles:
   (a) A way of killing ponies?
   (b) A contagious disease?
   (c) A vet's assistant?

10. Is Lockjaw:
    (a) A kind of twitch to keep horses quiet?
    (b) A horse's straightjacket?
    (c) Another name for Tetanus?

Picture Puzzle – Your First Aid Cupboard

Which of these items are not needed in your first aid cupboard?
The letters on the bottles are jumbled to make it harder.

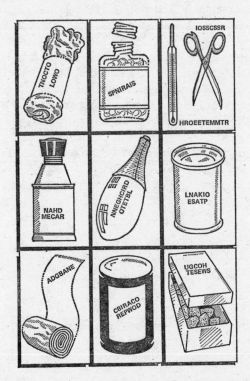

Quiz 40

Odd One Out

One word or phrase in each of these sets doesn't belong. Do you know which they are?

1. Anvil, Hammer, Screwdriver, Pincers.
2. Risen clench, Loose shoe, Cast shoe, Slip bar.
3. Ragwort, Privet, Yew, Cow Parsley.
4. Kaolin, Hoof oil, Animal lintex, Hot water.
5. Flat sided, Roarer, Broken winded, Whistler.
6. Bad teeth, Worms, Capped hock, Lice.
7. Cotton wool, Arsenic, Lint, Blunt-ended scissors.
8. Pawing, Weaving, Wind sucking, Crib biting.
9. Medicine, Bandages, Linctus, Marmite.
10. Racing plate, Tips, Fullered, Frilly.
11. Mange, Ringworm, Windgall, Sweet-itch.
12. Pricked foot, Frog, Nail binding, Bruised sole.

Right or Wrong?

Some of these statements are right, some wrong. Do you know which are which?

1. An anti-tetanus injection is given to prevent tetanus.
2. Acorns are not poisonous.
3. Thrush is an infection of the pastern.
4. Girth galls are caused by hard or dirty girths rubbing a pony's skin.
5. A pony's temperature is taken down his ears.
6. Pony Gout is another name for laminitis.
7. A pony vomits when he has eaten too much straw.
8. Sandcrack is caused by eating sand.
9. A pony should not drink stagnant water.
10. A sprained tendon causes lameness.
11. Worms make a pony's coat shine.
12. Humans can catch ringworm from ponies.

Pair Them Up
Do you know which of these words go together?

DRENCH   LINCTUS

HORSE

SALTS   COLIC   WIND   WOOL

EPSOM

COUGH   SHOE

SLIPPED   SPRAINED

HEELS

CRACKED   TENDON

SHOE   STIFLE

SHOEING   OVER

COTTON WORM CLENCH

DOSE   GIRTH

BITER   RISEN   SUCKER

COLD

GALL   CRIB   REACH

LOOSE

Fill in the Missing Words

choosing from amongst those at the bottom of the page

1. An ill pony should .... be ridden.
2. A very fat pony may get ....
3. There is .... cure for a broken wind.
4. Thrush is a disease of the ....
5. A twisted gut is often caused by neglected ....
6. If your pony scratches a lot he may have .... living in his coat.
7. If your pony cuts himself he will need an anti .... injection.
8. You should call the .... at once if your pony has colic.
9. Middle-aged ponies usually need their .... rasped.
10. A pony's normal temperature is .... than a human's.
11. Lame ponies need ....
12. A risen clench means that your pony's .... is becoming loose.
13. A blacksmith uses .... to make his fire burn better.
14. Stringhalt is a .... complaint.

nervous lice measles shoe no definitely vet
water bellows sunshine teeth rest fairies
colic laminitis remote tetanus ignoring not
frog tomato higher

Quiz 44

Anagrams

1. CEDHNR.
2. INLAV.
3. IMTSILANI.
4. NOKILA TAPES.
5. TBAMSLIKHC.
6. EBSINDEO.
7. OSELO ESOH.
8. HRTUSH.
9. ADESBNGA.
10. CEHLNC.

Quiz 45

Sort Them Out

In each section some suggestions are true, some are false. Can you pick out the true ones?

1. *SOS. Needs first aid treatment:*
   Broken knees? Bog spavin? Gaping wound? Arterial bleeding? Missing shoe? Cut fetlock? Sharp tooth? Slipped stifle? Bleeding side? Sickle hock?

2. *SOS. Vet at once:*
   Nappiness? Colic? Collapsed condition? Intermittent and irregular breathing? Splint? Capped Hock? Internal bleeding? Old age? High temperature?

3. *SOS. Vet:*
   Sprained tendon? Jibbing? Conjunctivitis? Stubbornness? Cow hocks? Cracked heels? Ewe neck? High crest? Saddle sore? Pointing a toe?

4. *SOS. Wrong feeding – change the diet:*
   Bad condition? Warbles? Sweet-itch? Seedy toe? Laminitis? Monday morning disease? Wind sucking? Goose-rump? Poisoning? Arthritis?

5. *SOS. Could be bad shoeing:*
   Corns? Poll evil? Faulty hocks? Thrush? Con-

tracted heels? Windgalls? Long toe? Brittle
hoof? Ringworm? Over-reach?

6. *SOS. Diseases of the foot:*
Ringbone? Broken wind? Side bone? Sinus?
Sand-crack? Cracked tendon? Navicular? Rheu-
matism? Canker? Mange?

7. *SOS. Serious illness:*
Pneumonia? Hernia? Stone in hoof? Tangled
legs? Influenza? Rubbed tail? Horse pox?
Ragwort poisoning? Girth gall? Bee sting?

8. *SOS. Blacksmith needed:*
Loose shoe? Round hoof? Prick? Cast shoe?
Fullered shoe? Displaced shoe? Stone in shoe?
Worn-through shoe? Grubby shoe? Worm in
shoe?

9. *SOS. Extra warmth needed (rugs etc):*
Newly clipped? Very ill? Mid-summer? High
temperature? New pony? Sprained fetlock?
Biting stable door? Very thin in winter? Newly
born? Shivering, with cold ears?

10. *SOS. Deadly dangerous:*
Yew? Sorrel? Swallowed plastic bags? Old grass
mowings? Hazel nut leaves? Meadow Sweet?
Lorries that don't slow down? Wilting ragwort?
Last year's hay? Blackberry leaves?

Ponies – Makes and Shapes

Story Puzzle

Why was Flash so difficult to ride?

'A good horse is never a bad colour,' said Mr Hargreaves, writing a cheque for two hundred pounds. 'I like a bay myself.'

David was delighted with Flash. He looked so strong and sturdy, with a huge neck, and a crest like an ancient warhorse. David was pale and underweight. He frequently had bouts of asthma. He never played games, but he had ridden a little on a friend's pony. Flash was said to be quiet and reliable, perfect in traffic, easy to catch, box and shoe.

The Hargreaves turned him out in a farmer's field and the next day David started riding him. At first everything went well, because Flash had been ridden by a girl with strong arms and a good nerve. But soon he started to take hold, and however hard David pulled on the reins, he wouldn't stop. Finally he galloped under a tree and the branches dragged David off. David never rode again and Flash was sent to a market where he was bought for meat.

What was wrong with Flash's conformation? Why was he so difficult to ride?

Quiz 47

Which One Fits?

1. Is a blaze:
   (a) A kind of jump?
   (b) A white marking stretching between the eyes and down to the nose?
   (c) A Mountain or Moorland stallion?

2. Is the Connemara:
   (a) The native pony of Ireland?
   (b) A Welsh pony?
   (c) A breed often seen in the New Forest?

3. Is tied-in below the knee:
   (a) A hobbled pony?
   (b) A fault in conformation?
   (c) A pony which needs bandages?

4. Is a Dorsal Stripe:
   (a) A stripe of white stretching from forehead to muzzle?
   (b) Stripes on a Zebra?
   (c) A dark or dun stripe stretching from withers to tail?

5. Should a pony's shoulder be:
   (a) Sloping?
   (b) Straight?
   (c) Very thin?

6. Is the Croup:
   - (a) A contagious cough?
   - (b) The point between the loins and the root of the tail?
   - (c) Another name for chest?

7. Is a Cob:
   - (a) A breed of pony?
   - (b) Another name for a docked tail?
   - (c) A type of horse or pony?

8. Is a Wall-eye:
   - (a) An eye pinkish-white or bluish-white in appearance?
   - (b) A diseased eye?
   - (c) A small mean eye?

9. Is the Gaskin:
   - (a) Another name for crest?
   - (b) Above the gullet?
   - (c) Also called the second thigh?

10. Is a Roan:
    - (a) A type of pony?
    - (b) A colour?
    - (c) A rogue horse?

Quiz 48

Picture Puzzle – Markings and Styles

Can you name the different markings and styles on this horse?

Quiz 49

Odd One Out

One word or phrase in every line doesn't fit. Can you find it?

1. Wavy, Dappled, Flea-bitten, Iron.
2. Highland, Shetland, Mull, Welsh.
3. Cannon bone, Pastern, Knee, Poll.
4. Donkey stripe, Star, Blaze, Snip.
5. Black, Bay, Piebald, Brown.
6. Ewe neck, Roach back, Sickle hocks, Short cannon bone.
7. Exmoor, Dartmoor, New Forest, Arab.
8. Straight Pastern, Boxy feet, Large eye, Long cannon bone.
9. Jack Ass, Mule, Jenny, Pony.
10. Dartmoor pony, Show, Jumping, Harness.
11. Pommel, Withers, Elbow, Croup.
12. Dun, Grey, Roan, Purple.

Quiz 50

Right or Wrong?

Some of these statements are right, some wrong. Do you know which are which?

1. A hollow back is a strong back.
2. All Shetland ponies have boxy hoofs.
3. A good horse is seldom a bad colour.
4. Dale ponies come from the North of England.
5. Grey ponies become whiter with age.
6. Cow hocks are the same as sickle hocks.
7. Connemara ponies are under 12.2 hh.
8. A wall-eye means a blind eye.
9. Icelandic ponies are strong and sturdy.
10. A large eye means a likely shyer.
11. Black ponies usually bite.
12. A liver chestnut is a pony which consumes liver.

Pair Them Up
Do you know which of these go together?

DORSAL   COLOURED   GOOSE

GALVEYNE'S

STRIPE   BLACK

BLUE   WELSH   GROOVE

ODD   ROAN

POINTS   BONE

CANNON   FETLOCK

STRING   EARS   NOSE

JOINT   FACE   HAM

GREY

RUMP   PIGEON   MOUTH

LOP   ROMAN

PARROT

TOED   DAPPLE

DISH   PONY

Quiz 52

Fill in the Missing Words

choosing from amongst those at the bottom of the page

1. A Welsh pony should have .... ears.
2. A hollow back is a sign of .... age.
3. Grey ponies become much .... when they are old.
4. An Exmoor pony should have a .... nose.
5. Some bay ponies have .... points.
6. .... inches make a hand.
7. A dorsal stripe is also called a .... stripe.
8. A black and white pony is called ....
9. A Palomino is usually .... in colour.
10. A show pony must not exceed .... hands in height.

golden   speckled   mealy   strawberry   donkey
old   wobbly   piebald   American   black   8 foot
whiter   14.2   odd   small   twenty   four   curly

Quiz 53

Anagrams

1. SRETC.
2. LBSAKDEW.
3. CLESKI SCOHK.
4. EMOXOR.
5. OPLMAONI.
6. SINGKA.
7. LENGIDG.
8. WEE CNEK.
9. KETOFLC.
10. ONTIP.

Quiz 54

Sort Them Out

In each section, some descriptions are true, and some are false. Can you pick out the true ones?

1. *British pony breeds:*
   Fell, Thoroughbred, Anglo Arab, Dartmoor, Shetland, Shire, Percheron, Dale, Suffolk Punch, Exmoor.

2. *Points of the Horse:*
   Gaskin, Gasket, Croup, Crock, Gullet, Mullet, Hamstring, Hammock, Beechnut, Chestnut.

3. *Recognized colours:*
   Blue roan, Red dun, Blue black, Bay, Cream, Yellow dun, Purple bay, Dappled grey, Spotted strawberry.

4. *Points of the hoof:*
   White line, Little toe, Grass tip, Frog, Sole, Sollex, Bars, Point of nail, Wall, Cliff.

5. *Accepted markings:*
   Snip, Blaze, Patch, Piece, Stripe, Ring, Star, Walleye, Pink eye, White blot.

6. *Joints:*
   Corns, Hock, Crest, Hamstring, Knee, Fetlock, Forelock, Stifle, Hip, Flank.

7. *Faults in conformation:*
   Straight shoulder, Short cannon bone, Goose rump,
   Long back, Thick neck, Sloping pastern, Deep girth,
   Small eye.

8. *Scottish ponies:*
   Highland, Isle of Man, Hill, Western Island, Valley,
   Shetland, Garron, Moor, Purple Heather, Barra.

9. *Breeds of horses:*
   Polo, Cleveland Bay, Arab, Cob, Shire, Clydesdale,
   Vanner, Coach horse, Thoroughbred, Hunter.

10. *Male ponies:*
    Colt, Filly, Mare, Stallion, Maiden, Entire, Gelding,
    Dam, Sire, Female.

Tack and Equipment

Quiz 55

Story Puzzle

Why did Starlight go berserk?

The twins had just been given a pony called Starlight. He was narrow chested and high withered with a small star on a beautiful head.

'Now we need some tack,' said their father. 'How about trying the market on Saturday? I don't suppose there's much difference between one saddle and another.'

'It must have a leather lining,' said Paul.

'And forward cut flaps,' added Patricia.

So on Saturday they all visited a nearby market and Horse sale. They soon found themselves bidding for a forward cut, leather-lined saddle and a pelham bridle. The saddle was eventually theirs for thirty pounds, the bridle for five.

On returning home the twins couldn't wait to try out the new tack on Starlight.

'Bags ride him first,' shouted Paul.

'Gosh he looks terrific in it!' exclaimed Patricia.

They had difficulty in doing up the curb chain as none of them had ever seen one before, but once this was done, the twins rode Starlight successfully for more than a week. Then in their own words, 'he went berserk', refusing to go forward, bucking and flinging his head from side to side.

Finally, in despair, they rang up Starlight's previous owner who immediately blamed the tack.

What was wrong with it? Why did Starlight go berserk?

Quiz 56

Which One Fits?

1. If you are showing your pony, should you ride him in:
   (a) A dressage saddle?
   (b) A forward cut saddle?
   (c) A straight cut saddle?

2. If your pony needs a rug for summer shows, should you buy him:
   (a) A Sweat rug?
   (b) A New Zealand rug?
   (c) A jute night rug?

3. If your stable doorway is very low, should you:
   (a) Hold your pony's head down when you lead him in?
   (b) Keep him tied up all the time so he won't bang his head?
   (c) Realize it's dangerous and do everything you can to make it higher?

4. If your stable has a very high hay rack which your pony can barely reach, should you:
   (a) Use a haynet instead?
   (b) Go on using it?
   (c) Put planks underneath for your pony to stand on?

5. If your wheelbarrow collapses when you are mucking out, should you:
   (a) Give up until you can make your parents buy another one?
   (b) Put lots of fresh straw on top of the dirty?
   (c) Use a sack split down the middle to carry away the muck and dirty straw?

6. If your pony's saddle slips back, should you buy:
   (a) A breastplate?
   (b) A crupper?
   (c) A Dee Martingale?

7. Is a Numnah:
   (a) A type of girth?
   (b) A rug worn under a night rug?
   (c) Used under a saddle?

8. Should webbing girths be cleaned by:
   (a) Scraping with a knife?
   (b) Using a special detergent kept by saddlers for the purpose?
   (c) Scrubbing with soap and water?

9. Does Neatsfoot oil:
   (a) Make leather more supple?
   (b) Make stirrups shine?
   (c) Keep your stable smelling sweet?

10. Is a rowel:
    (a) A ring attached to a bridoon?
    (b) Part of a spur?
    (c) A tool used for mucking out?

Picture Puzzle

Name the tack

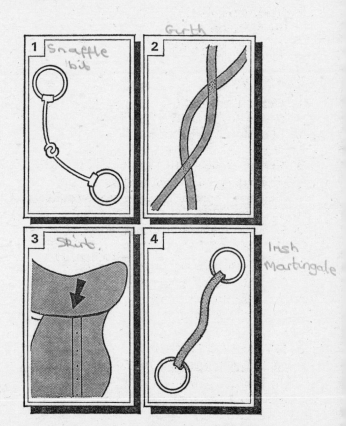

1 Snaffle bib

2 Girth

3 Skirt.

4 Irish Martingale

Quiz 58

Odd One Out

*One word or phrase in each of these groups doesn't belong. Do you
know which they are?*

1. Linen, Leather, Serge, Satin.
2. Girth, Stirrup leathers, Cheek strap, Breastplate.
3. Broom, Fork, Pick axe, Shovel.
4. Headcollar, Headstall, Halter, Bridle.
5. Noseband, Browband, Cantle, Headpiece.
6. Burnisher, Curry comb, Rubber, Body brush.
7. Scamperdale, Eggbutt, Jointed, Ring.
8. Exercise, Crepe, Tail, Back.
9. Scoop, Hoof pick, Feed bin, Bucket.
10. Saddle soap, Beeswax, Neatsfoot oil, Flexalan.
11. Eglantine, Nickel, Stainless steel, Silver.
12. Concrete, Staffordshire brick, Flints, Brick.

Quiz 59

Right or Wrong?

Some of these statements are right, some wrong. Do you know which are which?

1. A hoof pick is for picking out your pony's hoofs?
2. The best stirrups are made of plastic?
3. A salt lick is bad for ponies' teeth?
4. Any fool can repair a broken saddle tree?
5. A twisted snaffle is a very mild bit?
6. The stable rubber is for rubbing down the stable walls?
7. A dandy brush is for removing mud and dirt from your pony's coat?
8. Tail bandages are for sore tails?
9. Chaff is easily cut with cutting-out scissors?
10. A razor blade is excellent for trimming manes?
11. Shelters should be open in front to avoid accidents?
12. Large dustbins with lids are good for storing oats, bran, nuts, etc?

Quiz 60

Pair Them Up

Do you know which of these words go together?

DANDY   BREAST   PITCH   DROP

MANE   BRUSH

BARROW

WHEEL   FORK

OIL   TAIL

SUMMER   NET

CHEEK   STIRRUP

PLATE

COMB

SHEET   COLLAR

ROOM   BANDAGE   BIN

HEAD   LEATHERS

NOSEBAND   PIECE

HAY

BRACKET   TACK   SADDLE

HOOF

FEED

Quiz 61

Fill in the Missing Words

choosing from amongst those at the bottom of the page

1. A jumping saddle is usually .... cut.
2. A double bridle has .... bits.
3. A .... stops a saddle slipping forward.
4. .... straw is the best straw for bedding.
5. Old ponies often cannot eat .... oats.
6. A wisp is made out of plaited ....
7. A .... comb is used for cleaning the body brush.
8. Rubber stirrup .... will stop your feet slipping.
9. A .... snaffle is a very mild bit.
10. A .... noseband will stop your pony opening his mouth too wide.

whole   rubber   missing   treads   butter   clamps
curry   nylon   wheat   ragwort   hay   winter
crupper   reverse   forward   drop   scottish   two
eighteen

Quiz 62

Anagrams

1. DEBILR.
2. OFOH CIKP.
3. SHERANS.
4. HTICP RFKO.
5. FESFANL.
6. PRUCREP.
7. DELSDA ROHES.
8. RASWT.
9. TALSEB BREBUR.
10. MOLEPM.

Quiz 63

Sort Them Out

In each section some suggestions are true, and some are false. Can you pick out the true ones?

1. *Points of the saddle:*
   Rib? Cantle? Pommel? Round flap? Skirt? Seat? List? Lining? Butt?

2. *Points of the bridle:*
   Ear piece? Browband? Nose strap? Throat lash? Cheek piece? Bit strap? Reins? Eye band? Noseband? Back rein?

3. *Types of snaffles:*
   Gag? Scamperdale? Jointed? Curb? Rubber? Pelham? Port? Fulmer? Half moon? Vulcanite?

4. *Points of a double bridle:*
   Port? Weymouth bit? Bridoon bit? Gag strap? Curb chain? Third rein? Throat chain? Curb rein? Martingale buckle? Drop noseband?

5. *Martingales:*
   Stopping? Standing? Hanging? Irish? Flat? Running? Cheshire? Berkshire? Pulley? Showing?

6. *Clothing for clipped and stabled pony:*
Headdress? Night rug? Stable bandages? Gamgee? Tail bandage? Day rug? Churn strap? Surcingle or roller? Morning rug? Afternoon roller?

7. *Clothing for you:*
Jodphurs? Shorts? Riding boots? Strap shoes? Crash cap? Riding jacket? Chin strap? Woolly gloves? Spotted neck tie? Under-cap?

8. *Useful equipment:*
Saddle bracket? Midden shed? Tack room? Bridle hook? Hoof pick stand? Fork cupboard? Saddle horse? Weighing machine? Hay tin? Bandage roller?

9. *More useful equipment:*
Lunging rein? Trotting rein? Leading rein? Gag halter? Head collar? Riding whip? Oat grinder? Tail strap? Knee caps? Glass feed bin?

10. *Types of saddles:*
Bucking? Showing? Mountain? Dressage? Trekking? Felt? Jumping? Running? Racing? Camp?

Breeding – Buying and Selling

Quiz 64

Story Puzzle
Why did no one want Smoky?

Smoky was a small grey four-year-old. He belonged to Andrew, who was twelve and needed money for a new camera. Andrew advertised Smoky in the local paper as suitable for beginners, hoping to be paid two hundred pounds. He didn't mention his age nor that Smoky was liable to buck. Several people answered the advertisement and tried Smoky. The children were all small and inexperienced. Smoky ran away with the first and bucked off the second. Then he was sent away on trial, but was soon returned with his reputation in ruins – he had broken a child's neck. Now no one wanted Smoky, and Andrew was unable to buy a new camera.

What did Andrew do wrong? Why did no one want Smoky?

Quiz 65

Which One Fits?

1. A Brood mare is:
   (a) A broody mare?
   (b) A mare used for breeding?
   (c) An old mare?

2. A Vet's Certificate means:
   (a) That your pony has been passed as quiet by a vet?
   (b) That he's been innoculated by a vet?
   (c) That he has been passed as sound by a vet?

3. If you sell a pony as sound, which has had laminitis, are you:
   (a) Breaking the law?
   (b) Being clever?
   (c) Being a good horse coper?

4. If you have a pony on trial, should you:
   (a) Take him to as many shows as possible?
   (b) Appreciate he isn't yours and use him sensibly?
   (c) Ask all your friends round to give their opinion?

5. If your mare is in foal, should you:
   (a) Hunt her?

(b) Stop riding her after a month or two and give her extra food?

(c) Turn her out to fend for herself?

6. If you can't manage your new pony, should you:
   (a) Send him to a horse sale?
   (b) Ring up his previous owners and shout at them?
   (c) Blame yourself and seek expert advice?

7. If you are selling a vicious pony, should you:
   (a) Sell him as safe for little children?
   (b) Sell him to a friend and have the last laugh?
   (c) Tell the truth and sell him to someone who can cope?

8. Does a newly born foal:
   (a) Suck milk from his Dam (mother)?
   (b) Need a bottle?
   (c) Need bran mash and codliver oil?

9. Are newly born foals:
   (a) Hidden by their Dam for a few days?
   (b) In need of a New Zealand rug?
   (c) Soon cantering about?

10. Is the Sire:
    (a) The father of a foal?
    (b) A young stallion?
    (c) The horse knights rode?

Picture Puzzle

Can you name the bad points in conformation?

Quiz 67

Odd One Out

One word or phrase in every line doesn't fit. Can you find it?

1. Anglo-Arab, Half-bred, Crossbred, Three-quarter bred, Thoroughbred.
2. Roaring, Windsucking, Laminitis, Napping, Lameness.
3. Gestation, Foaling, Weaving, Weaning, In foal.
4. Auction, Shop, Sale, Market, Dealer's yard.
5. Plait, Oil hoofs, Pull tail, Dock tail, Groom.
6. Crib biting, Bolting, Rearing, Trotting, Traffic shy.
7. Splints, Spavins, Goose rump, Curb, Capped hock.
8. Boxy hoofs, Round hoofs, Cracked hoofs, Split hoofs, Shallow hoofs.
9. Very old, Too small, Rather fat, Too strong, Like an elephant.
10. Much too large, Ignorant, Unkind, Untidy, Mad.
11. Vet, Soldier, Horsebox driver, Stud groom, Stables.
12. Insult, Praise, Pat, Reward, Ride.

Quiz 68

Right or Wrong?

Some of these statements are right, some wrong. Do you know which are which?

1. Mares in foal should not be allowed any exercise.
2. Very young foals need plenty of maize.
3. Your own vet should never vet a pony you are selling.
4. A pony on trial should never be ridden.
5. If a mare does not foal quickly, you should call a vet.
6. A mare in foal needs good food.
7. A mare may have to visit a stallion several times before she is in foal.
8. A pony without any sort of warranty is always a risky buy.
9. Pigeon toes are an unsoundness.
10. Foals always grow larger than their dams.
11. Weedy foals are healthy foals.
12. Old mares are often difficult to get in foal.

Quiz 69

Pair Them Up
(There are three 'ands' to help you.)

TROT   DEALER'S

STUD   AND

            BROOD   TRIAL

    BOOK   HORSE

DEALER

       FOALING   CERTIFICATE

              STUD   DAM

FAIR   AND

   BOX

           OUT   HORSE

   FARM

      FOAL   MARE   MARE

YARD   ON   AND

        SELL

  VET'S

     AT   IN

        SIRE

    BUY

FOAL   STUD

Quiz 70

Fill in the Missing Words

choosing from amongst those at the bottom of the page

1. The mother of a foal is called his ....
2. The father of a foal is called his ....
3. Sometimes you are allowed a pony on ....
4. A horse is not sound if he is .... in the wind.
5. A mare used for .... is called a brood mare.
6. When a pony is examined for a vet's certificate, he is usually .... to test his wind.
7. When buying a pony you can tell his age by his ....
8. An old pony often has a .... back.
9. The average time a mare is in foal is .... months.
10. The usual age for weaning a foal is .... months.

twenty trial parent breeding track sire tail
hollow hiring eleven dam bold gone
whistling teeth annoyed six aunt galloped
scared

Anagrams

1. ASFLO.
2. OREHS LESA.
3. ISINBHPOG.
4. TUSD.
5. TEVTDE.
6. TINASLOL.
7. CEVSI.
8. RSHOE NAD ONHDU.
9. REMA.
10. RRAWTAN.

Quiz 72

Sort Them Out

In each section some suggestions are true, and some are false. Can you pick out the true ones?

1. *Bad place to sell beloved pony:*

   At auction? At horse sale? At home? At horse show? At abbattoir? At market? On farm? At friend's place? At riding school? At knackers?

2. *Ways of cheating buyers:*

   Plaiting mane? Putting boot polish on scars to hide them? Selling pony prone to sweet-itch in winter? Oiling hoofs? Doping to make placid? Re-shoeing? Giving pain killers to hide lameness? Bishoping? Plaiting tail? Exercising?

3. *Nasty way to sell pony:*

   Deceitfully? Carefully? Truthfully? Dishonestly? For eating? When thin and exhausted? To good home? When very old? With consideration for future of pony? With consideration for new owners?

4. *Suitable treatment for newly born foal:*

   Leading lessons? Dosing with Epsom Salts? Plenty of peace and quiet? Curry combing? A warm bed? Plenty of shade or shelter? Quiet confident handling? Schooling in a covered school? Mouthing bit to be used like a baby's dummy? Encouragement to suck from dam if needed?

5. *Suitable treatment for mare in foal:*
Feed extra vitamins? Warm shelter or stable made available? Plenty of work? Plenty of clean water? Plenty of excitement? Frequent galloping? Constant dosing with Epsom Salts? Great care? Extra food towards end of pregnancy? To be tied up tightly before foaling?

6. *Suitable treatment for stallion:*
To be kept in the dark? To have regular exercise? To be treated with great caution like a bull? To be well fed? To have ring placed in nose? To be kept docile by starving? To have hoofs picked out daily? To wear bit day and night? To be treated kindly? To be groomed regularly?

7. *Suitable home for old pony:*
As companion to other horses? Hiring stable? For riding by someone equally old? Busy trekking centre? As pet to knowledgeable people? For really small children? Large pony-less family of keen riders? As school master to young ponies? As point-to-pointer? For cats' meat?

8. *Ways of increasing value of pony you wish to sell:*
By clipping? By trimming? By teaching to rear? By schooling? By lending to incompetent friends? By riding fast on hard roads? By riding successfully at shows? By correct feeding? By getting splints and spavins? By teaching to overbend?

9. *Ways of impressing would-be buyers:*
By showing photographs of pony with rosettes pinned to his bridle? By showing off own great knowledge of ponies? By laughing at their ignorance? By offering drinks? By asking double what you want? By talking non-stop? By telling them everything you know about pony? By leaving them time to talk things over among themselves? By having pen ready to sign cheque? By putting on best clothes?

10. *The right way to behave when viewing a pony:*
Run down pony? Sneer at tack? Be polite? Ask addresses of previous owners? Try to sound superior? Explain what you want pony for? Tell them about Daddy's Rolls? Insist on a vet's certificate? Tell them about all the prizes you have won? Be nice to pony?

Uses of Horses – Past and Present

Quiz 73

Story Puzzle
What was wrong with Patrick's ride?

It was the year 1802. The Ostler was getting Master Patrick's hunter ready. He put on a forward cut jumping saddle with a nylon girth, and an eggbutt snaffle bridle with rubber reins. He then attached a bearing rein and waited for Master Patrick who soon appeared dressed in jeans, rubber riding boots and an Acrilan jersey.

Patrick mounted quickly, riding away down the tarmac drive without saying thank you. His hunter had had a great many pony cubes and was difficult to manage. He slipped on the tarmac road and shied at the shiny dustbins put out for the corporation dust cart. Soon Patrick met the stage coach which was pulled by nine horses. The coachman blew his bugle shouting, 'Get out of the way'. So Patrick returned home swearing at his hunter which was now bleeding profusely from the mouth, his tongue having been cut by the action of the cruel bearing rein.

This story is full of mistakes. How many can you find?

Quiz 74

Which One Fits?

1. Is a polo pony:
   (a) Used for a game called polo?
   (b) Used for advertisements for polo mints?
   (c) A roly poly pony?

2. Was a charger:
   (a) A horse which charged at people?
   (b) A horse ridden many years ago by policemen charging people?
   (c) A war horse?

3. Was a tandem:
   (a) A kind of bicycle pulled by ponies?
   (b) Two harness horses driven one in front of the other?
   (c) A pole used for rapping lazy jumpers?

4. Was a palfrey:
   (a) A riding habit for a lady?
   (b) A Welsh pony?
   (c) A medieval small, lightweight saddle horse?

5. Are Liberty horses:
   (a) Horses which like to be free?
   (b) A type of specially trained circus horses?
   (c) An American breed?

6. Were cab horses used to pull:
   (a) Buses?
   (b) Trams?
   (c) Cabs?

7. Was a cockhorse:
   (a) An extra horse used on steep hills to help other horses pull their loads to the top?
   (b) A cocky horse with lots of 'go'?
   (c) A horse soldiers rode when their guns were cocked ready for action?

8. Was a pad-horse:
   (a) A horse which moved quietly?
   (b) The second horse in a tandem?
   (c) An ancient term for an easy-paced horse used for riding on the road?

9. Is a pace-maker:
   (a) A horse which sets the pace in a race?
   (b) Another name for a pacer?
   (c) An ancient breed of pony?

10. Did Fell ponies in the past:
    (a) Pull stage coaches?
    (b) Compete in jousting matches?
    (c) Carry lead from the mines to the sea?

Picture Puzzle

Join the dots.

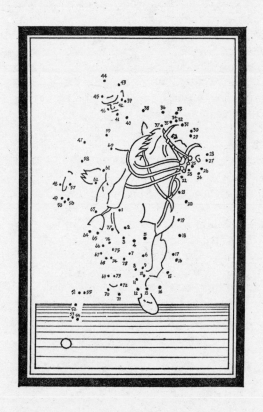

Quiz 76

Odd One Out
One word or phrase in every line doesn't fit. Can you find it?

1. Steeple chasing, Polo, Flat racing, Point-to-pointing.
2. Trekking centre, Riding school, Gymnastic centre, School of equitation.
3. Wheeler, Cleveland bay, Tandem, Pair.
4. Charger, Hunter, Hack, Hackney.
5. Show jumper, Eventer, Leading rein pony, Working pony.
6. Circus horse, Dressage horse, High school horse, Stallion.
7. Carriage horse, Cock horse, Coach horse, Cockroach.
8. Carriage horse, Cab horse, Omnibus horse, Tram horse.
9. Hay cutter, Tractor, Hay rake, Waggon.
10. Dray, Dog cart, Waggonette, Jeep.
11. Tanks, Guns, Ambulances, Food supplies.
12. Sire, Stallion, Dam, Filly.

Quiz 77

Right or Wrong?

Some of these statements are right, and some are wrong. Do you know which are which?

1. Horses were once used to pull canal barges.
2. Pegasus was the winged horse of Greek myth.
3. Alexander the Great rode Bucephalus.
4. Stage coaches first ran in 1902.
5. Man o' war was one of the first great show jumpers.
6. The white Lipizzaners of Austria are the ballet dancers of the horse family.
7. The Pony Express was named after the famous stallion – 'Express'.
8. Thoroughbreds are not allowed to race on a 'Hat track'.
9. Postillions rode on cock horses.
10. In the past butchers were known for their high-stepping harness horses and ponies.
11. Before clipping became fashionable horses sometimes died of exhaustion in the hunting field.
12. Liberty horses are circus horses controlled by the ring master.

Quiz 78

Pair Them Up

Do you know which of these words go together? There are two 'ands' to help you

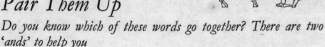

HORSE   SCHOOL

PIT   CART

JUMPER

DRESSAGE   HORSE

PONY

COACH   CARRIAGE

BROOD

POLO

PONY   MARE   FOUR

AND   PAIR

HIGH

RIDING   POLICE

COCK

AND   MATCH   WAR

TREK

HORN   SCHOOL

ARENA   HORSE

COACHING SHOW HORSE

Quiz 79

Fill in the Missing Words

choosing from amongst those at the bottom of the page

1. Years ago most carriage horses stood in ....
2. The cavalry rode .... into battle.
3. A Trandem is .... horses driven abreast, also known as a Manchester team.
4. Very well schooled horses usually compete in .... tests.
5. Years ago all cart horses had their tails ....
6. A Phaeton was pulled by .... ponies.
7. Horses used to pull canal ....
8. Working ponies are expected to .... when competing.
9. Horses once pulled Hansoms which were two-wheeled ....
10. Race horses are always ....
11. Heavyweight hunters must be able to carry .... riders.
12. There are still a few ponies working underground in British ....
13. There are lots of .... matches at Windsor.
14. Horses used to pull hearses were always ....

jump barges polo crossbred two stalls
ponies cabs fields piebald carts three
heavy black horses four docked pits
dressage thoroughbred

Quiz 80

Anagrams

1. ITP OYPN.
2. RECA ESHOR.
3. ACOHC.
4. INUTNHG.
5. OLPO.
6. SOJTUS.
7. RVINDGI.
8. LGUPOH.
9. TABLET.
10. HKACUK.

Quiz 81

Sort Them Out

In each section, some suggestions are true, and some are false. Can you pick out the true ones?

1. *A Horse Trial horse needs:*
   Courage? A strong neck? Small hoofs? Jumping ability? Stamina? High withers? A goose rump? Fitness? Good ears? Schooling?

2. *A first pony must be:*
   Patient? Fast? Quick? Quiet? Reliable? Thoroughbred? Well-schooled? Under five? Good-tempered? Very strong?

3. *Years ago, horses pulled:*
   Barges? Milk carts? Steam rollers? Trucks in mines? Bulldozers? Haycutters? Combine harvesters? Traction engines? Trams? Trolley buses?

4. *Polo ponies must be:*
   Long backed? Flat footed? Handy? Quick off the mark? Arab? Sound? Fast? Taught how to play? Weight carriers? 14 hands high?

5. *Dressage horses need:*
   Great stamina? To be supple? Good action? Great strength? Flat knees? Cadence? Large heads? Much schooling? Good riders? Slim legs?

6. *Ponies working in the coal pits were:*
Stallions? Exmoors? Geldings? From Iceland?
Cobs? Shetlands? Three year olds? Helped by
mules? Clipped all over including mane and tail?

7. *Years ago pack ponies carried:*
Milk? Eggs? Lead? Peat? Slates? Bricks?
Concrete? Tin? Fruit? Coal?

8. *Cabs were:*
Often pulled by worn-out carriage horses? Like
buses? For hire? With their drivers sitting outside? Mostly in towns? On moors? Seen outside
railway stations? Invented in 1409? Called after
Lord Cab?

9. *The Lipizzaners at the Spanish Riding School in Vienna
perform:*
Over jumps? The Capriole? Across country? The
Courbette? Polo? The Levade? As Working
hunters? The Mug race? The Piaffe? High school
movements?

10. *The Pony Express was:*
A fast mail service? Capable of covering nearly
2,000 miles in ten days? In Russia? In America?
Ridden in stages? A train service? In England? A
mail service from St Joseph, Missouri to San Francisco? Something to do with the Canadian Moun-
ties? A police force?

Crosswords

Crossword No 1

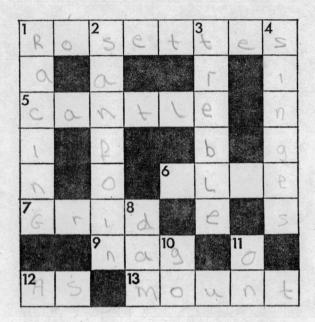

¹R	o	²s	e	t	³t	e	⁴s
a		a			r		i
⁵c	a	n	t	l	e		n
l		f			b		g
i		o		⁶	l		e
⁷G	r	i	⁸d		e		s
		⁹n	a	¹⁰g		¹¹o	
¹²A	s		¹³m	o	u	n	t

Across

1. Won at shows (8)
5. Back of a saddle (6)
6. — roan (4)
7. A row of small jumps (4)
9. Slang word for a horse (3)
12. — hounds ran (2)
13. To get on a horse (5)

Down

1. Usually on television on Saturday afternoons (6)
2. A kind of hay (7)
3. A combination of three jumps (6)
4. She — the coat when burning off the remaining hair after clipping (6)
8. Mother of a foal (3)
10. On your marks, get set, — (2)
11. Get —. Get off (2)

Crossword No 2

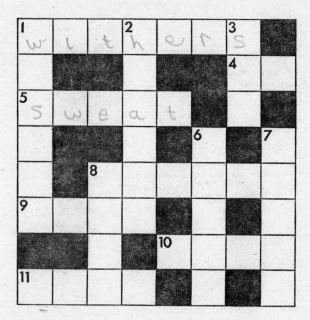

Across

1. Stops the saddle slipping forward (7)
4. Rack — (2)
5. Your pony does this after he's been ridden (5)
8. Hay is put in this (6)
9. Four-in-hand can be called this (4)
10. Artificial aid (4)
11. A jump (4)

Down

1. A tit-bit (6)
2. A bit (6)
3. Night — (3)
6. Small white markings (5)
7. — and finish (5)
8. Stop (4)

Crossword No 3

Across

1. One of the phases in Horse trials (8)
5. Part of the grooming kit (6)
7. — cart (3)
9. Royal — (4)
11. Ears which flop downwards are called this (3)
13. If your pony is seriously — you should call the vet at once (3)
14. You can't jump — the moon (4)
15. The underground home of a fox (5)

Down

1. A mountain and moorland breed (8)
2. Point of the horse (5)
3. Your pony should — his winter coat in spring and get a summer one (4)
4. — neck (3)
6. Keeps the rug in place (6)
8. — well up to bridle (2)
10. The father of a foal (4)
12. You may ride along this through a wood (4)

Crossword No 4

Across

1. Part of the bridle (8)
4. A bruise in the sole region (4)
5. A two wheeled carriage (3)
6. An artificial scent (4)
7. Dark — night (2)
8. A horse may jump out at a bag in the road (3)
10. — salt (4)
11. Left side (4)
12. — harness (2)

Down

1. Kicks up hindlegs (5)
2. — greys (7)
3. The noise a horse makes (5)
5. Part of the hind leg (6)
7. A breed (4)
9. Area outside the stables (4)
11. Initials for National Hunt (2)

Crossword No 5

Across
1. Blacksmith (7)
5. Manner of sitting horse (4)
6. Keeps saddle in place (5)
7. — reaching (4)
9. 3 jumps in a — make a treble (3)
10. — hand (2)
12. Part of the hind leg (4)
14. Run away out of control (4)

Down
1. Part of foot (4)
2. Makes noise when galloping (6)
3. One of two found on the horse's head (3)
4. — coat (7)
5. At these you will find jumping classes, gymkhana events etc (5)
8. Refuse to go forward (3)
11. Do grey horses get darker in colour as they grow older? (2)
13. Initials for Hampshire Hunt (2)

Answers

Quiz 1

Because Sally gave him far too little to eat. Ponies need at least 12 lbs of hay a day in winter; much more than you can carry in a shopping basket! Potato peelings are not a suitable food, and a cupful of porridge oats is no more than a titbit.

Quiz 2

1. (b).
2. (c).
3. (b).
4. (c).
5. (a).

6. (c).
7. (c).
8. (b).
9. (a).
10. (b).

Quiz 3

A and 4.
B and 2.

C and 1.
D and 3.

Quiz 4

1. Silage.   The others are types of hay.
2. Meadow.   The others are used for straw.
3. Broken.   The others are types of oats.
4. Hay.   The others are all classed as 'hard feed'.
5. Schooling. The others are all to do with his coat and appearance.
6. Foot.   The others are types of clips you can give your pony.

7. Wrenching. The others are all ways of treating a mane.

8. Sack up. The others are all done while grooming and mucking-out.

9. Kicking. The others are all to do with grooming.

10. Roads. The others should all be checked before putting your pony in a new field.

11. Flour. The others are all fed to horses in some form or other.

12. Hysterically. The others are all the right way to treat your pony. Hysterically is not!

Quiz 5

1. Wrong – you should never bring in a pony hot, but should walk the last mile to cool him off unless it is raining.

2. Right.

3. Wrong – ponies don't like hot water.

4. Wrong – most lame ponies need complete rest.

5. Right.

6. Right.

7. Wrong – musty hay is extremely bad for ponies and will do harm to any pony coughing or suffering from bronchitis.

8. Right.

9. Wrong – your pony should always have water available. A long drink after a feed can wash oats into the intestines, causing colic.

10. Right.

11. Right.

12. Wrong – no pony needs that many oats.

Quiz 6

Bran mash, hogged mane, crushed oats, full clip, muck out, tack up, rub down, flaked maize, boiled linseed, turn out, bang tail, rug up, trace clip, pony nuts, salt lick.

Quiz 7

1. Ice.
2. Rugs.
3. Day.
4. Fences.
5. Dry.
6. Galloped.
7. Never.
8. Not.
9. Twice.
10. Every.

Quiz 8

1. Linseed.
2. Halter.
3. Stabled.
4. Hunter clip.
5. Fence.
6. Mucking out.
7. Bran mash.
8. Grooming.
9. Chaff.
10. Staring coat.

Quiz 9

1. Pony nuts. Mixture hay. Grass. Chopped carrot. Crushed oats.
2. Dandy brush. Water brush. Body brush. Stable rubber. Curry comb.
3. Saddle soap. Sponges. Neatsfoot oil. Metal polish. Soft duster.
4. Loose box. Farmer's field. Shady paddock. Stable. Orchard.
5. Bring in all day in summer. Visit every day. Pick out hoofs before riding. Examine shoes regularly. Clean his tack regularly.

6. Remove dung. Keep water trough clean. Inspect fences regularly. Fill up rabbit holes. Pick up garbage and sharp stones.
7. Peat. Sawdust. Wood shavings. Wheat straw. Oat straw (not as good as wheat).
8. Increase food. Worm. Get teeth examined. Have examined by vet. Feed boiled linseed, soaked flaked maize and boiled barley.
9. Meadow hay. Grass. Crushed oats. Bran. Extra vitamins.
10. Give less food. Ride regularly. Bring in every day in summer. Put in smaller field. Ride slowly until thinner.

Quiz 10

No. Ann should have been disqualified for knocking down a pole in the bending, but might have won a fourth rosette if there were only four competitors in the final.

In the potato race, she should have thrown the potato in the bucket from her pony's back and finished mounted.

In the musical poles, Ann should have been sent out because she failed to hold on to the pole: not the girl on the skewbald pony.

Quiz 11

1. (a).	6. (b).
2. (b).	7. (a).
3. (a).	8. (c).
4. (c).	9. (c).
5. (b).	10. (b).

Quiz 12
Answers: 4 and 6.

Quiz 13
1. Spoon and Fork.   Others are recognized gymkhana competitions.
2. Get on and off.   Others are recognized jumping events.
3. Vanguard.   Others are show jumps.
4. Ordinary   Others are pony showing classes.
5. There and Back.   Others are recognized gymkhana competitions.
6. Grade G.   Others are recognized jumping grades.
7. Jumping at Hickstead   Others are all events, mostly across country.
8. Iceland.   Others all have International Show Jumping teams.
9. Musical Paperbags. Others are all recognized variations of gymkhana competitions.
10. Apple Bobbing.   Others are all competitions with two or more riders.
11. River.   Others are all possible jumps when competing. (You can only ford a river.)
12. Gate.   Others are all jumps made up of poles.

Quiz 14
1. Right.
2. Wrong – you must belong to the Pony Club.
3. Wrong – many horses don't reach their peak until later.

4. Wrong – there is no junior class at Badminton.
5. Right.
6. Right.
7. Right.
8. Right.
9. Right.
10. Right.
11. Wrong – passing a flag on the wrong side usually means elimination.
12. Wrong – you should *always* wear a hard hat when riding.

Quiz 15
Hunter trials, rustic poles, musical sacks, apple bobbing, late entry, steeple chasing, mug race, challenge cup, scurry jumping, handy hunter, collecting ring, shark's teeth, bronze medal, false start, clear round.

Quiz 16
1. Open.
2. Saddle.
3. Derby.
4. Wembley.
5. Five.
6. Show jumps.
7. Three.
8. Refusal.
9. Eliminated.
10. Coat; gloves.
11. Combination.
12. Young.

Quiz 17
1. Show ring.
2. Triple.
3. Schedule.
4. Jumping.
5. Hickstead.
6. Arena.
7. Irish Bank.
8. Plaits.
9. Bullfinch.
10. Water jump.

Quiz 18

1. Sack race. Fancy dress. Bending race. Musical poles. Trotting race.

2. Novice jumping. Local jumping. Scurry competition. Hit and hurry. Open jumping.

3. Mountain and Moorland. First pony. Leading rein. Family pony. Working pony. Best child's pony not over 13.2.

4. Hunter. Hack. Working hunter. Brood mare. Arab.

5. To be plaited (but not for Mountain and Moorland classes). A straight cut saddle. Clean tack. To lead in hand. A tidy rider.

6. A double bridle. To be plaited. To jump. To be well groomed. A good rider.

7. Apples. Buckets. Poles. Potatoes. Flags.

8. Run and lead. Balloon race. Stepping stones. Dressing-up race. Anti-litter race.

9. A serpentine. Circles. Leads off on either leg. Standing still. Ordinary trot sitting.

10. Water jump. Rustic poles. Gate. Road closed. Triple.

Quiz 19

Ponies should never be jumped much on hard ground, nor should they be jumped every day. Twice a week is usually plenty for a schooled pony. Jumps should be changed around so that a pony doesn't become bored. Twilight stopped jumping because her legs were jarred by the hard ground, and she had been jumped far too much.

Quiz 20

1. (b).
2. (a).
3. (c).
4. (b).
5. (c).

6. (b).
7. (a).
8. (c).
9. (a).
10. (a).

Quiz 21

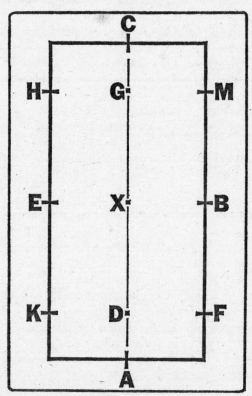

DIAGRAM OF DRESSAGE ARENA

Quiz 22

1. Stop.   Others are paces.
2. Somersault.   Others are to do with getting on and off.
3. Peculiar.   Others are variations of trot or canter.
4. Spurs.   Others are natural aids; spurs are artificial.
5. Half-rear.   Others are schooling exercises.
6. Flexing.   Others are bad habits.
7. Dropping the nose.   Others are ways of evading the bit.
8. Stiffly.   Others are virtues in a schooled pony.
9. Lazily.   Others are the way in which *you* should ride!
10. Balanced.   Others are bad habits.
11. On the bit.   Others are more ways of evading the bit.
12. Long gallops.   Others are balancing exercises.

Quiz 23

1. Right.
2. Wrong – you should sit in the centre of your saddle.
3. Right.
4. Wrong – the walk is a four time gait.
5. Wrong – dressage horses must be able to lead off on either leg.
6. Wrong – your hands should be just above and in front of your saddle.
7. Wrong – so much schooling quickly sours a pony.
8. Right.
9. Wrong – he should stand square when he halts.
10. Right.

11. Right.
12. Right.

Quiz 24
Spread fence, lunge rein, rising trot, leg up, falling off, rein back, breaking in, collected canter, school master (the horse variety), mouthing bit, run out, ground line, flying change, counter canter (wrong leg leading), artificial aids.

Quiz 25
1. Down.
2. Aids.
3. Inside.
4. Loose.
5. Martingale.
6. Artificial.
7. Sitting.
8. Rewards.
9. Lose.
10. Stirrups.

Quiz 26
1. Trotting.
2. Rein-back.
3. Aids.
4. Rally.
5. Jumps.
6. Half pass.
7. Gallop.
8. Shoulder-in.
9. Circle.
10. Canter.

Quiz 27
1. Is kind but firm. Has heels lower than toes. Looks between his pony's ears. Is straight without being stiff. Uses his brains.

2. Improve your pony. Make him balanced. Make him easier to ride. Make him better at competitions. Increase his value.

3. Has a hard mouth. Needs schooling. Is badly ridden. Has wrongly adjusted bit. Is too strong for his rider.

4. Lacks training. Is sore or lame. Is constantly jagged in the mouth. Can't jump such a big fence. Is being ridden by a nervous rider.

5. His saddle pinches. He suffers from a cold back. He's had too many oats. He wants his own way. He needs more exercise.

6. Turns on the haunches. Circling. Turns on the forehand. Stopping and starting. Half halts.

7. Rising. Ordinary. Collected. Extended. Sitting.

8. Jibbing. Bolting. Rearing. Napping. Kicking other ponies.

9. Balances your pony. Gets your pony fit. Muscles up your pony's quarters. Gets his hocks under him. Improves him for Horse Trials.

10. Quiet hacking. Work he will enjoy. Taking slowly until he's five. Plenty of leg. Not too much of anything until he's five.

Quiz 28
Because Ann Moore is alive now. Sir Alfred Munnings has been dead for some time and Anna Sewell lived at a different time altogether, and wrote only one book, *Black Beauty*. *My Friend Flicka* was written much more recently by Mary O'Hara.

Quiz 29

1. (a).	6. (b).
2. (b).	7. (a).
3. (c).	8. (c).
4. (a).	9. (a).
5. (c).	10. (c).

Quiz 30

Writer: Monica Edwards.
Commentator: Dorian Williams.
Jockey: Pat Taaffe.
Painter: George Stubbs.
Polo player: Prince Charles.
Show Jumper: Ted Edgar.

Quiz 31

1. Esther Rantzen. — The others are authors.
2. Anneli Drummond-Hay. — The others jump for the USA.
3. Alice in Wonderland. — The others are pony books.
4. Dorian Williams. — The others are cartoonists or illustrators.
5. Crusader. — Others are famous show jumpers.
6. Virginia Wade. — Others are famous show jumping riders.
7. The Rock (Italian horse). — Others have jumped for Great Britain.
8. Vibart (Show jumper). — Others are horses in books.

9. David Broome.

Others are famous trainers.

10. Tommy Wade.

Others are famous jockeys.

11. William Carson.

Others are famous Horse Trial riders.

12. Christine.

Others are characters in *Follyfoot*.

Quiz 32

1. Right.
2. Wrong – he is a show jumping rider.
3. Wrong – Pitz Palu is ridden by Alan Oliver.
4. Right.
5. Wrong – Monica Dickens wrote *Follyfoot*.
6. Wrong – George Hobbs has never ridden round Badminton.
7. Right.
8. Right.
9. Wrong – Alan Oliver is a show jumping rider.
10. Right.
11. Right.
12. Right.

Quiz 33

Mark Phillips. Ann Moore. Harvey Smith. Dorian Williams. Princess Anne. Monica Dickens. George Stubbs. Alan Oliver. David Broome. Hans Winkler. Lester Piggott. Marion Mould. Dick Turpin. Anna Sewell. Richard Meade.

Quiz 34

1. McMahon.
2. Great.
3. Piggott; flat.
4. Harvey Smith.
5. Black Beauty.
6. Marengo.
7. Munnings.
8. Polo.
9. Pat Smythe.
10. Mother.

Quiz 35

1. David Broome.
2. Arkle.
3. Mary O'Hara.
4. Stubbs.
5. Doublet.
6. Mark Phillips.
7. Lester Piggott.
8. Psalm.
9. Pegasus.
10. Anna Sewell.

Quiz 36

1. Pat Smythe. Gillian Baxter. Joanna Cannan. Mary Gervaise. Josephine Pullein-Thompson.
2. Richard Meade. Mary Gordon-Watson. Princess Anne. Mark Phillips. Sheila Wilcox.
3. Stephen Hadley. Marion Mould. Peter Robeson. Alison Dawes. Bill Steinkraus.
4. Merrylegs. Flicka. Cavalier. Black Bess. Snowcloud.
5. R. S. Summerhays. Henry Wynmalen. The Duke of Newcastle. Caprilli. Golden Gorse.
6. Grebe. Red Admiral. Foxhunter. April Love. Stroller.
7. Roberto. Nijinsky. Hyperion. Mill Reef. Golden Miller.
8. Doublet. Cornishman V. Rock On. Be Fair. Great Ovation.
9. Red Alligator. Highland Wedding. Red Rum. Ayala. Foinavon.
10. Mr Banbury. Mr Softee. Top of the Morning. Summertime. Hideaway.

Quiz 37

Susan should have known that many paints contain lead and are deadly poisonous. She should have removed the empty tins and asked the men to stop throwing them over the fence. She should have sent for a vet as soon as she knew that Daydream was ill. Daydream died because he licked out the paint left in the tins, because Susan didn't send for the vet in time, and because a girl of ten is much too young to look after a pony on her own.

Quiz 38

1. (c).
2. (a).
3. (c).
4. (a).
5. (b).
6. (c).
7. (c).
8. (a).
9. (b).
10. (c).

Quiz 39

Aspirins, hand cream, cough sweets.
You should have: bandage, scissors, horse thermometer, cotton wool, boracic powder, and kaolin paste.

Quiz 40

1. Screwdriver.   The others are tools used by a blacksmith.
2. Slip bar.   The others are all concerned with shoes falling off.
3. Cow Parsley.   The others are poisonous or deadly to ponies.
4. Hoof oil.   The others are used for fomenting or reducing swellings.
5. Flat sided.   The others are complaints affecting a pony's breathing.

6. Capped hock. The others affect a pony's general condition.
7. Arsenic. The others should be in your medicine box. Arsenic should NOT!
8. Pawing. The others are nervous complaints.
9. Marmite. The others are used by a vet.
10. Frilly. The others are types of shoes.
11. Windgall. The others are all skin complaints.
12. Frog. The others are all causes of lameness.

Quiz 41

1. Right.
2. Wrong – acorns, the bark and leaves of an oak tree are poisonous to a pony, though not usually fatal.
3. Wrong – thrush is a disease of the frog.
4. Right.
5. Wrong – a pony's temperature is taken up his rectum.
6. Right.
7. Wrong – ponies cannot vomit.
8. Wrong – sandcrack is a split in the wall of the hoof.
9. Right.
10. Right.
11. Wrong – worms damage a pony's condition and health.
12. Right.

Quiz 42

Crib biter, cough linctus, horse shoe, epsom salts, loose shoe, sprained tendon, slipped stifle, cracked heels, cotton wool, worm dose, risen clench, wind sucker, cold shoeing, girth gall, over reach, colic drench.

Quiz 43

1. Not.
2. Laminitis.
3. No.
4. Frog (foot or hoof ½ a mark)
5. Colic.
6. Lice.
7. Tetanus.
8. Vet.
9. Teeth.
10. Higher.
11. Rest.
12. Shoe.
13. Bellows.
14. Nervous.

Quiz 44

1. Drench.
2. Anvil.
3. Laminitis.
4. Kaolin paste.
5. Blacksmith.
6. Sidebone.
7. Loose shoe.
8. Thrush.
9. Bandages.
10. Clench.

Quiz 45

1. Broken knees. Gaping wound. Arterial bleeding. Cut fetlock. Bleeding side.
2. Colic. Collapsed condition. Intermittent and irregular breathing. Internal bleeding. High temperature.

3. Sprained tendon. Conjunctivitis. Cracked heels. Saddle sore. Pointing a toe.

4. Bad condition. Sweet-itch. Laminitis. Monday morning disease. Poisoning.

5. Corns. Contracted heels. Long toe. Brittle hoof. Over-reach.

6. Ringbone. Side bone. Sand-crack. Navicular. Canker.

7. Pneumonia. Hernia. Influenza (can be serious with horses). Horse pox. Ragwort poisoning.

8. Loose shoe. Prick. Cast shoe. Displaced shoe. Worn-through shoe.

9. Newly clipped. Very ill. High temperature. Very thin in winter. Shivering, with cold ears.

10. Yew. Swallowed plastic bags. Old grass mowings. Lorries that don't slow down. Wilting ragwort.

Quiz 46
Because he had a huge thick neck which made him very strong and likely to be headstrong. David was weak and needed a much lighter pony.

Quiz 47

1. (b).	6. (b)
2. (a).	7. (c).
3. (b).	8. (a).
4. (c).	9. (c).
5. (a).	10. (b).

Quiz 48
Answers: 1. Stripe. 2. Ermine Marks. 3. Stocking. 4. Bang Tail. 5. Hogged mane. 6. Pulled Tail.

Quiz 49

1. Wavy. — Others are types of grey.
2. Welsh. — Others are Scottish breeds.
3. Poll. — Others are points on legs.
4. Donkey stripe. — Others are markings on head.
5. Piebald. — Others are principal colours; piebald is odd-coloured.
6. Short Cannon bone. — Others are faults in conformation.
7. Arab. — Others are British Mountain and Moorland breeds.
8. Large eye. — Others are faults in conformation.
9. Pony. — Others are to do with donkeys!
10. Dartmoor pony. — Only one breed of pony.
11. Pommel. — Others are points of horses. Pommel is a saddle point.
12. Purple. — Others are accepted colours of horses.

Quiz 50

1. Wrong – a hollow back is usually caused by age.
2. Wrong – most Shetlands have good feet.
3. Right.
4. Right.
5. Right.
6. Wrong – cow hocks are hocks turning inwards.
7. Wrong – Connemara ponies usually stand 13–14 hands high.
8. Wrong – wall-eyes do not denote blindness.
9. Right.
10. Wrong – a large eye usually means a kind pony.
11. Wrong – black ponies can be as nice as other ponies.
12. Wrong – liver chestnut is a colour.

Quiz 51

Dorsal stripe, odd coloured, galveyne's groove, blue roan, black points, fetlock joint, cannon bone, hamstring, pigeon toed, parrot mouth, lop ears, roman nose, dish face, dapple grey, welsh pony, goose rump.

Quiz 52

1. Small.
2. Old.
3. Whiter.
4. Mealy.
5. Black.
6. Four.
7. Donkey.
8. Piebald.
9. Golden.
10. 14.2.

Quiz 53

1. Crest.
2. Skewbald.
3. Sickle Hocks.
4. Exmoor.
5. Palomino.
6. Gaskin.
7. Gelding.
8. Ewe neck.
9. Fetlock.
10. Pinto.

Quiz 54

1. Fell, Dartmoor, Shetland, Dale, Exmoor.
2. Gaskin, Croup, Gullet, Hamstring, Chestnut.
3. Blue roan, Bay, Cream, Yellow dun, Dappled grey.
4. White line, Frog, Sole, Bars, Wall.
5. Snip, Blaze, Stripe, Star, Wall-eye.
6. Hock, Knee, Fetlock, Stifle, Hip.
7. Straight shoulder, Goose rump, Long back, Thick neck, Small eye.
8. Highland, Western Island, Shetland, Garron, Barra.
9. Cleveland Bay, Arab, Shire, Clydesdale, Thoroughbred.
10. Colt, Stallion, Entire, Gelding, Sire.

Quiz 55

Like your shoes, saddles must fit.

A high-withered pony needs a well padded saddle. The twins and their father needed an expert to advise them. A wrongly adjusted curb chain can make a sore quite quickly. Starlight went berserk because he had a sore chin groove, sore withers and a sore back, all caused by ill-fitting or wrongly adjusted tack.

Quiz 56

1. (c).
2. (a).
3. (c).
4. (a).
5. (c).
6. (a).
7. (c).
8. (c).
9. (a).
10. (b).

Quiz 57

1. Eggbutt Snaffle. 2. Balding Girth. 3. Skirt. 4. Irish Martingale.

Quiz 58

1. Satin.	The others are all used as saddle linings.
2. Cheek strap.	The others are attached to the saddle.
3. Pick axe.	The others are used for mucking out.
4. Bridle.	The others do not have bit attached.
5. Cantle.	The others are part of a bridle.
6. Burnisher.	The others are grooming tools.
7. Scamperdale.	A pelham, the others are types of snaffle.
8. Back.	The others are types of bandages used for horses.

9. Hoof pick. The others are all connected with feeding.

10. Beeswax. Not normally used for cleaning tack like the others!

11. Silver. All the other metals are used for bits and stirrups.

12. Flints. All the others are used for stable floors.

Quiz 59

1. Right.
2. Wrong – plastic is an unsuitable material for stirrups.
3. Wrong – all ponies need minerals contained in a salt lick.
4. Wrong – it needs an expert to repair a broken tree.
5. Wrong – a twisted snaffle is severe because of rough edges and nutcracker action.
6. Wrong – the stable rubber is for polishing your pony.
7. Right.
8. Wrong – a tail bandage is to keep a pulled tail looking smart.
9. Wrong – the scissors will be ruined.
10. Wrong – manes should be pulled.
11. Right.
12. Right.

Quiz 60

Dandy brush, wheel barrow, breast plate, pitch fork, mane comb, summer sheet, stirrup leathers, cheek piece, head collar, drop noseband, hay net, feed bin, tack room, saddle bracket, tail bandage, hoof oil.

Quiz 61

1. Forward.
2. Two.
3. Crupper.
4. Wheat.
5. Whole.
6. Hay.
7. Curry.
8. Treads.
9. Rubber.
10. Drop.

Quiz 62

1. Bridle.
2. Hoof pick.
3. Harness.
4. Pitch fork.
5. Snaffle.
6. Crupper.
7. Saddle horse.
8. Straw.
9. Stable rubber.
10. Pommel.

Quiz 63

1. Cantle. Pommel. Skirt. Seat. Lining.
2. Browband. Throat lash. Cheek piece. Reins. Noseband.
3. Gag. Jointed. Rubber. Fulmer. Half moon. Vulcanite.
4. Port. Weymouth bit. Bridoon bit. Curb chain. Curb rein.
5. Standing. Irish. Running. Cheshire. Pulley.
6. Night rug. Stable bandages. Tail bandage. Day rug. Surcingle or roller.
7. Jodphurs. Riding boots. Crash cap. Riding jacket. Chin strap (to keep crash cap on).
8. Saddle bracket. Tack room. Bridle hook. Saddle horse. Weighing machine.
9. Lunging rein. Leading rein. Head collar. Riding whip. Knee caps.
10. Showing. Dressage. Felt. Jumping. Racing.

Quiz 64

Andrew should not have advertised Smoky as suitable for beginners as most four-year-olds are unreliable. Smoky should have been advertised as needing an experienced rider, particularly as he was liable to buck. Andrew ruined Smoky's good name by trying to sell him to unsuitable people. Once Smoky had broken a child's neck, no one wanted him.

Quiz 65

1. (b).
2. (c).
3. (a).
4. (b).
5. (b).
6. (c).
7. (c).
8. (a).
9. (c).
10. (a).

Quiz 66

Goose-rump. Ewe neck. Small eyes. Big ears. Parrot mouth. Shallow hoofs. Sickle hocks.

Quiz 67

1. Thoroughbred.	The others are crossbred not pure bred.
2. Napping.	The others are all a type of unsoundness and should be mentioned on any vet's certificate.
3. Weaving.	The others are all to do with breeding.
4. Shop.	The others are all places where you could buy or sell a horse.
5. Dock tail (an illegal practice)	The others are all things you could do to improve your pony's appearance before selling.

6. Trotting.   The others are all vices or faults which should be avoided when buying a pony.

7. Goose rump.   The others are all swellings or enlargements which should be examined by a vet before buying.

8. Round hoofs.   The others should be carefully considered before buying, as they are liable to cause unsoundness.

9. Rather fat.   Others can never be changed.

10. Untidy.   Others are unsuitable purchasers for your pony.

11. Soldier.   Others are all likely to be found working around Stud farm.

12. Insult.   The others are all things you can or should do when showing off your pony to likely buyers.

Quiz 68

1. Wrong – they should have gentle exercise.
2. Wrong – very young foals live on their dam's milk.
3. Wrong – but a would-be buyer would do better to use his own vet.
4. Wrong – a pony is sent on trial for you to try.
5. Right.
6. Right.
7. Right.
8. Right.
9. Wrong – pigeon toes are a fault in conformation.
10. Wrong – not if they are poorly fed or have much smaller sires.
11. Wrong – weedy foals are always suspect.
12. Right.

Quiz 69

Stud book, foaling box, on trial, trot out, stud farm, brood mare, horse dealer, vet's certificate, horse fair, mare and foal, buy and sell, sire and dam, in foal, at stud, dealer's yard.

Quiz 70

1. Dam.
2. Sire.
3. Trial.
4. Gone.
5. Breeding.
6. Galloped.
7. Teeth.
8. Hollow.
9. Eleven.
10. Six.

Quiz 71

1. Foals.
2. Horse Sale.
3. Bishoping.
4. Stud.
5. Vetted.
6. Stallion.
7. Vices.
8. Horse and Hound.
9. Mare.
10. Warrant.

Quiz 72

1. At auction. At horse sale. At abbattoir. At market. At knackers.
2. Putting boot polish on scars to hide them. Selling pony prone to sweet-itch in winter. Doping to make placid. Giving pain killers to hide lameness. Bishoping.
3. Deceitfully. Dishonestly. For eating. When thin and exhausted. When very old.

4. Plenty of peace and quiet. A warm bed. Plenty of shade or shelter. Quiet confident handling. Encouragement to suck from dam if needed.

5. Feed extra vitamins. Warm shelter or stable available. Plenty of clean water. Great care. Extra food towards end of pregnancy.

6. To have regular exercise. To be well fed. To have hoofs picked out daily. To be treated kindly. To be groomed regularly.

7. As companion to other horses. For riding by someone equally old. As pet to knowledgeable people. For really small children. As school master for young ponies.

8. By clipping. By trimming. By schooling. By riding successfully in shows. By correct feeding.

9. By showing photographs of pony with rosettes pinned to his bridle. By offering drinks. By telling them everything you know about pony. By leaving them time to talk things over by themselves. By having pen ready to sign cheque.

10. Be polite. Ask addresses of previous owners. Explain what you want pony for. Insist on a vet's certificate. Be nice to pony.

Quiz 73

An Ostler worked at Inns and Taverns, not at private houses. Jumping saddles, nylon girths, eggbutt snaffles, rubber reins, tarmac roads, jeans, rubber riding boots, Acrilan, shiny dustbins, pony cubes and corporation dustcarts did not exist in 1802. Bearing reins were not used on riding horses, nor were stage coaches pulled by nine horses. The coachman would have blown a horn, not a bugle.

18 mistakes in all!

Quiz 74

1. (a).	6. (c).
2. (c).	7. (a).
3. (b).	8. (c).
4. (c).	9. (a).
5. (b).	10. (c).

Quiz 75

Join the dots: Polo pony and rider.

Quiz 76

1. Polo.	Others are races.
2. Gymnastic Centre.	Others are all places where you can ride ponies.
3. Cleveland Bay.	Others are all positions in harness for driven horses.
4. Hackney.	The only one used in harness.
5. Leading rein pony.	Others are all expected to jump when competing.
6. Stallion.	Others need high degree of training.
7. Cockroach.	Not a horse!
8. Carriage Horse.	Others all provided transport for anyone able to pay the fare.
9. Tractor.	Others pulled by horses in the past.
10. Jeep.	Others pulled by horses in the past.
11. Tanks.	Others pulled by horses in past wars.
12. Filly.	Others are parents, or used for breeding.

Quiz 77

1. Right.
2. Right.
3. Right.
4. Wrong – they were one of the main forms of transport long before that!
5. Wrong – he was a great race horse.
6. Right.
7. Wrong – it carried mail at great speed, hence the name.
8. Wrong – registered thoroughbreds can race on a 'Hat track'.
9. Wrong – they rode on carriage horses.
10. Right.
11. Right.
12. Right.

Quiz 78

Pit pony, show jumper, cart horse, pony trek, cock horse, coach and four, brood mare, polo match, riding school, carriage and pair, coaching horn, dressage arena, war horse, police horse, high school.

Quiz 79

1. Stalls.
2. Horses.
3. Three.
4. Dressage.
5. Docked.
6. Two.
7. Barges.
8. Jump.
9. Cabs.
10. Thoroughbred.
11. Heavy.
12. Pits.
13. Polo.
14. Black.

Quiz 80

1. Pit pony.
2. Race horse.
3. Coach.
4. Hunting.
5. Polo.
6. Jousts.
7. Driving.
8. Plough.
9. Battle.
10. Chukka.

Quiz 81

1. Courage. Jumping ability. Stamina. Fitness. Schooling.
2. Patient. Quiet. Reliable. Well-schooled. Good-tempered.
3. Barges. Milk carts. Trucks in mines (often called tubs). Haycutters. Trams.
4. Handy. Quick off the mark. Sound. Fast. Taught how to play.
5. To be supple. Good action. Cadence. Much schooling. Good riders.
6. Stallions. Geldings. From Iceland. Shetlands. Clipped all over, including mane and tail.
7. Lead. Peat. Slates. Tin. Coal.
8. Often pulled by worn-out carriage horses. For hire. With their drivers sitting outside. Mostly in towns. Seen outside railway stations.
9. The Capriole. The Courbette. The Levade. The Piaffe. High school movements. (They are high school horses.)
10. A fast mail service. Capable of covering nearly 2,000 miles in ten days. In America. Ridden in stages. A mail service from St Joseph, Missouri to San Francisco.

Crosswords

No 1

Across   1. Rosettes. 5. Cantle. 6. Blue. 7. Grid. 9. Nag. 12. As. 13. Mount.

Down   1. Racing. 2. Sanfoin. 3. Treble. 4. Singes. 8. Dam. 10. Go. 11. On.

No 2

Across   1. Crupper. 4. Up. 5. Rolls. 8. Haynet. 9. Team. 10. Spur. 11. Gate.

Down   1. Carrot. 2. Pelham. 3. Rug. 6. Snips. 7. Start. 8. Halt.

No 3

Across   1. Dressage. 5. Rubber. 7. Dog. 9. Mews. 11. Lop. 13. Ill. 14. Over. 15. Earth.

Down   1. Dartmoor. 2. Elbow. 3. Shed. 4. Ewe. 6. Roller. 8. Go. 10. Sire. 12. Path.

No 4

Across   1. Browband. 4. Corn. 5. Gig. 6. Drag. 7. As. 8. Shy. 10. Rock. 11. Near. 12. In.

Down   1. Bucks. 2. Windsor. 3. Neigh. 5. Gaskin. 7. Arab. 9. Yard. 11. NH.

No 5

Across   1. Farrier. 5. Seat. 6. Girth. 7. Over. 9. Row. 10. In. 12. Shin. 14. Bolt.

Down   1. Frog. 2. Roarer. 3. Eye. 4. Staring. 5. Shows. 8. Jib. 11. No. 12. HH.

If you have enjoyed this PICCOLO Book, you may like to choose your next book from the titles listed on the following pages.

More About Horses From Piccolo

Christine Pullein-Thompson

A PONY SCRAPBOOK (illus)   25p
A SECOND PONY SCRAPBOOK
(illus)   25p

Two very lively anthologies of stories, articles, cartoons, puzzles and crosswords all about horses. Books which are really good to have on wet days when you have little to do. They'll stop you driving everyone mad! They won't know you're there!

Monica Dickens

FOLLYFOOT   20p
DORA AT FOLLYFOOT   20p

Two fascinating books of horse-stories at Follyfoot Farm, based on the Yorkshire Television series. Whether you are horse-mad or not you will find these adventures really gripping, and you will be surprised what can happen!

More From Monica Dickens

THE HOUSE AT WORLD'S END
(illus)   20p
SUMMER AT WORLD'S END
(illus)   20p
WORLD'S END IN WINTER (illus) 20p

While their father is sailing single-handed
round the world and their mother is in hospital,
the Fielding children – Tom, Carrie, Em and
Michael – determine to live by themselves
rather than stay with niggling relatives in a
grey London suburb. They settle down in
World's End, a deserted, tumbledown country
pub, and they soon find themselves caring for
all kinds of animals in distress, from a broken-
down horse to a wounded dog and even a lost
monkey (as well as having to deal with human
problems!). Their thrilling – and sometimes
dangerous – adventures are excitingly told in
these three books.

And Finally Some True Animal Stories

Ernest Dudley

RUFUS: THE STORY OF A FOX
(illus)   25p

Rufus, born in the wild Scottish Highlands,
was just six months old when he came into the
possession of Don MacCaskill, a local forester.
This is the unique true story of a wild creature
accepting captivity.

Eric Delderfield

TRUE ANIMAL STORIES (illus)   25p
**THE SECOND BOOK OF TRUE
ANIMAL STORIES** (illus)   25p

The world of animals is full of surprises and
here are two fascinating books with absorbing
stories about every kind of animal and about
safari parks and lion reserves. For instance,
read about the deep friendship between a hen
and a cat! and many other funny, sad, puzzling,
and amazing stories.